CAN THESE BONES LIVE

How the Providence of God Established America!

David P Pett

DEDICATED –

—⁓⁓⁓—

To those who contributed to my burden for History and the Church, including:

Dietrich Bonhoeffer, who knew the only way Germany could be saved, would be if Adolf Hitler lost and the Allies won. For this he prayed – and his prayer was answered! Hitler had Bonhoeffer hanged twenty-one days before his own suicide but in the end, Bonhoeffer won!

Jonathan Edwards and George Whitefield, whose unlimited devotion to Jesus Christ and great love for the world brought a Great Spiritual Awakening to America!

The fifty-six signers of the Declaration of Independence!

My Father and Mother, Reinhold and Margaret Pett, who taught me respect for the Word of God!

My wife Evelyne who fully understands my burden, and bore with me in the preparation of this manuscript!

Many others – you know who you are – who await their eternal reward!

CAN THESE BONES LIVE

CONTENTS

~~~

PREFACE

O ur adventure begins in Medieval England. The year was 1620! Under the authority of the Crown and supported by investors, the Mayflower set sail for an assigned destination in Virginia territory. But their sails were adjusted by the winds of God, taking them 400 miles north to the land of God's choosing. Of the 102 aboard, thirty-five were Pilgrims fleeing the tyranny of England; the rest were either sailors or investors. Their new land eventually became New England. Their ultimate mission became one of capturing an untamed region of majestic mountains, forests, plains and rivers, a frontier of abundance.

Of the original number, forty-seven died during the first devastating winter in their new land. When Captain Jones offered to take the remaining members back to England the next spring, none took up his offer. They had found their home! None of them could know that 150 years hence the eighteen families would be thirteen colonies; and the thirteen colonies would in time become one mighty nation, there to bless the world with its Christian approach to life.

A look at the last three centuries reveals the agonies and joys that led to eventual success in establishing **One Nation under God!** Certainly the first settlers could not see this! Today there is a disappointing decline in the culture that made America great. The foundations our Forefathers laid are crumbling. Though Rights and Freedoms granted by God are unchangeable, government snatches away as many as possible from the minds of Americans, sometimes purposefully; sometimes inadvertently.

Our study of History is crucial! On the 100th anniversary of the signing of the Declaration of Independence, in 1876, A.W. Foljambe said, **"The more thoroughly a nation deals with its history, the more decidedly will it recognize and own an over-ruling Providence."**[1]

Historical documents make several things clear: First, Christian Liberty was incompatible with the medieval ways of Europe. Second, there is a Biblical Standard to be sought and adopted for our culture. Third, there is a God of Providence who oversees man in his search for Truth and favorably lends his wisdom and strength to the man who seeks His face. God has no favorable relationship with men except through Jesus Christ. Fourth, the nations of the world have been given to Jesus Christ [Psalm 2:8], they belong to Him: He is the world's rightful King [2:6] and the entire world is designed to serve Him [2:11; Revelation 4:11].

He rules the world compassionately by means of Four Mandates: Government, Family, Culture and the Church. Each is directly under His authority and care. God's purpose for the world is two-fold: Jesus Christ changes the hearts of men by His death and resurrection, bringing man back into fellowship with Himself. Jesus Christ also changes the culture, which we will see clearly.

God's plan is linear, not cyclical: It has a beginning, a progression and an ending. As we travel through Historic Documents we will look at that plan from various angles. With anticipation – we study the past to discern the future – and in the process, we seek to understand why the bones are dead – and what it will take to bring them back to life.

INTRODUCTION

T he prophet Ezekiel writes: *"The hand of the Lord was upon me, and He carried me out in the Spirit and set me down in a valley full of bones. He caused me to pass among them:, behold, there were very many in the open valley and, lo, they were very dry. He said to me: 'Son of man, can these bones live?' And I answered: 'O Lord God, Thou knowest.'*

"Again He said to me, Prophesy over these bones and say: Behold, I will cause breath to enter into you and you shall live. And I will lay sinews and flesh upon you and cover you with skin—and you shall know that I am the Lord.

"So I prophesied as commanded and there was a noise and a shaking, and the bones came together: Bone to bone! And lo, the sinews and flesh came upon them – but there was no breath in them.

"Then the Lord said to me: Prophesy and say to the wind: Thus saith the Lord God: O breath – breathe upon these slain that they may live. As I prophesied breath came into them and they came

to life and stood on their feet, an exceeding great army." [Ezekiel 37:1-10]

Ezekiel's answer to the Lord's question seems hesitant: **"O Lord God, Thou knowest!"** He hesitated to say, **"No, they cannot live!"** for he was talking to the Almighty. Nor was he prepared to say **"Yes"** for that might have seemed arrogant: He left it in the Hand of Providence who answers not with words but with action: The once dry bones become a mighty army! *"These bones,"* God said to the prophet, *"represent the whole house of Israel."*

For the purpose of this book, **<u>Can These Bones Live</u>**, Ezekiel's bones represent America!

We live in a deteriorating world. Men live to the age of about 75; woman to the age of 80. Early in life, however, the aging process sets in until – toward the close of life – the heart is unable to sustain life. We assume that a society MUST accept a similar aging process until the time comes when life cannot be sustained. Because deterioration is gradual, we live with it. If it happened suddenly we would quickly seek the help of a specialist. Had America shifted suddenly from a Biblical foundation to an anti-Christian base in a short period of time, a second American Revolution would have quickly and decisively corrected the flaw. At least, that is the character of the men who began the great American experiment!

Being a man I would not understand the labor pains of childbirth. However, the longer I carry the burden of what I see happening in America, with so few bothering to look at the unnatural aging process, the more I begin to understand a mother's pain. She, of course, always has the joyous anticipation of holding a newborn baby to her heart. As for me . . . . . I shall console myself in knowing that the God of Providence is not dead!

SECTION I –

THE BACKBONE OF
COLONIAL AMERICA

The basic framework for the human body is the backbone. Through its core flows the entire nervous system that controls bodily functions. Imagination is enough to tell us what would happen if the body had no backbone. The body politic is having that problem today!

Time has a way of burying information in the recesses of our mind. This is especially true if the information we gathered seems unimportant. The farmer remembers, of course, how and when to plow, plant and harvest! Computer savvy is important for the entrepreneur or the would-be successful businessman. However, of what value is it to know why Pilgrims came to America? It seems so unimportant to know this; it does not relate to where we are in our modern consumer culture carried along by motivational seminars and positive preachers. Is it really important for us to know what education was like on the frontier, or if Washington and Adams believed in Jesus Christ?

This first Section considers aspects of Colonial life as understood by our American Founders. This is America's Backbone! We need to know what was important to them—and why! If it was so vital that it affected the way they set up their Government, should it be of any interest to us today? We need to know!

1 – PROVIDENCE IN COLONIAL AMERICA

Noah Webster defined Providence as, **"The care and superintendence which God exercises over his creatures. Some persons admit a general providence, but deny a particular providence, not considering that a general providence consists of particulars. A belief in divine providence is a source of great consolation to good men. By divine providence is understood God Himself."**[2]

Consider two aspects to the Providence of God: First, as it led to the discovery and founding of America; and second, as it was understood by America's Founders.

Our modern world struggles to explain historic events: How Israel crossed the Red Sea; how Noah's Ark landed on Mount Ararat; Jonah and the big fish; and the physical Resurrection of Jesus from death. The modern man attempts to extract these from the American mind, or else he must embrace it all as the work of Providence. While men today look back through the lens of time and make grand explanations, those who lived at the time understood the events to be the result of God's personal involvement. **This is Providence, and Providence bans accidents!**

Consider the direction taken by the Gospel: Inasmuch as the Holy Spirit is the Lord of the harvest [Matthew 9:38], it was no accident that the Gospel moved Westward, and Paul was chosen by God to spearhead that move. Sometime after his conversion Paul joined the believers in Antioch, and that Church sent him and Barnabas on a missionary tour. [Acts 13:1ff] When he determined to go north to Asia the Spirit stopped him. When he chose to go east to Bithynia *"the Spirit of Jesus did not permit it."* Then God gave Paul a vision of a man of Macedonia calling: *"Come and help us!"* Paul understood this to be the leading of the Spirit [Acts 16:6-10] and he headed West eventually reaching Rome. From there the Gospel ultimately spread to Europe, England and ultimately America, all under the Hand of Providence.

The year was 1492, right in the center of a momentous time, when Christopher Columbus sailed for America. Columbus trusted in the Providence of God, as he describes in his own words: **"It was the Lord who put into my mind (I could feel His hand upon me) . . . There is no question that the inspiration was from the Holy Spirit, because He comforted me with rays of marvelous inspiration from the Holy Scriptures . . . I have found the sweetest consolation since I made it my whole purpose to enjoy His marvelous presence. No one should fear to undertake any task in the name of our Savior, if it is just and if the intention is purely for His holy service."[3]**

Around 1450 John Guttenberg invented the printing press. In 1492 Columbus discovered America. In 1517 Martin Luther nailed his 95 theses to the Wittenberg Church door, challenging Rome's sale of the forgiveness of sins. And in 1534 King Henry VIII of England renounced Rome, declaring him to be the Head of the Church of England, taking with him all of Rome's personnel and property located in England. He named himself head of the Church of England, but was still the same scoundrel as before. Even in this Providence was at work: The more the King tried to control his people, the more they hungered for liberty.

Being under the King of England provided no more liberty of conscience than being under the pope of Rome. Consider one of Henry's children by the name of Mary who ruled England from 1553 to 1558. She chose to take the Church of England back under the authority of Rome. To do this she forced Englishmen to renounce Protestantism and give up their Bibles. Those who were born again believers could not in good conscience comply. So, about 300 Christians were burned to death by Bloody Mary, as she came to be called. **Foxe's Christian Martyrs of the World** tells the story of two men who were burned at the stake: Hugh, a lame man and John, a blind man. After being arrested they were called before the Bishop where they refused to deny their faith in Jesus Christ. They were both sentenced to burn at the stake. Arriving at the stake, Hugh threw away his crutches and said to his blind friend: **"Be of good comfort, brother, for the bishop of London is our good physician: he will cure us both shortly, thee of thy blindness and me of my lameness."[4]** These two old men were then chained to the stake and cheerfully yielded their lives for their faith.

Mary's successor, Queen Elizabeth, reversed Mary's Romish intentions. The pope had no soldiers or ships at his command, so he appealed to Spain to recapture England for him. If successful, Pope Sixtus V would pay Spain a large sum of money. So in 1588 Spain gathered more than 100 ships and thousands of men to attack England, but they were utterly destroyed – by an act of Providence. This is how it happened: Before 1588, England had used up all her trees in the making of ships, so they could no longer make ships out of wood. The answer: Invent a steel ship! As the battle with the Spanish Armada ensued, the steel ships that rode low in the water were poor targets for the tall wooden ships of Spain, while the Spanish ships were easy marks for the British. One after another the Spanish ships were sunk, while the low-lying iron ships came away unscathed. By the destruction of the Spanish Armada, Though the pope had given North and South America to Spain and Portugal in 1494, that gift was meaningless. Providence had other things in mind: England now ruled the high seas: Christian Pilgrims could freely travel to the New World without Spanish obstruction.

The British were more like Rome than like true Protestants: Five years after defeating the Spanish Armada, the British passed the Conventicle Act that required separatists to join the Church of England or be exiled or, is some cases, be executed. This too was Providential, for it catapulted the Pilgrims out of England in 1620: They could not bear to live under British repression. Though it was a stormy voyage, there were no Spanish ships to disrupt their crossing to Freedom and the New World in 1620. Such was the Providential Hand of God.

Consider the Providence of God as understood by America's Founders. George Washington said in his Inaugural Address on April 30, 1789 that **". . .it would be peculiarly improper to omit in this first official act my fervent supplications to that Almighty Being who rules over the universe, who presides in the councils of nations, and whose providential aids can supply every human defect. . . No people can be bound to acknowledge and adore the Invisible Hand which conducts the affairs of men more than those of the United States. . ."[5]**

Washington may have had in mind a number of striking events of his life: He may have been thinking of the new Constitution and the installation of a gold standard which solved a monetary crisis about to destroy individuals and the nation as well. Three years after the Constitution was signed, recalling those tragic days, Washington said, because of the new Constitution, serenity now reigns to such an extent that had someone foretold of that tranquility, **it would have been considered a species of madness.**

Or, did Washington have in mind the sinking of the Spanish Armada in 1588, referred to above? Had the Spanish won, Spain and Rome would have ruled our shores.

Perhaps Washington was thinking of 1746, the year the entire French Fleet prepared to ravish the Colonies. On October 16th of that year, as the French Fleet stood offshore waiting to attack, a destructive storm struck the fleet which had eluded our British protectors [America was then a British Colony].

Unknown to the French, America had called for a day of fasting and prayer ten days earlier, to be held on October 16th. On that very day the final storm all but wiped out Captain Duc d'Anville and his ships. For three days the Captain waited in a dense fog; when it lifted a devastating sight lay before his eyes. Few ships remained. Unable to report his failure back home in France, he committed suicide, as did his successor. The third in command staggered back to France with a few ships still afloat, warning his country, **"Do not fight the Colonies; God fights for them!"**

This event was superbly captured by Henry Wadsworth Longfellow in his poem, ***The Ballad of the French Fleet***. It was written by Longfellow as though it was composed by Thomas Prince, pastor of Boston's Old South church, expressing what many Americans felt at the time.

A fleet with flags arrayed
Sailed from the port of Brest;
And the Admiral's ship displayed
The signal: "Steer southwest."
For this Admiral D'Anville
Had sworn by cross and crown
To ravage with fire and steel
Our helpless Boston Town.

There were rumors in the street,
In the houses there was fear
Of the coming of the fleet,
And the danger hovering near.

And while from mouth to mouth
Spread the tidings of dismay;
I stood in the Old South,
Saying humbly: "Let us pray!"

"O Lord! We do not advise;
But if, in Thy Providence
A tempest should arise
To drive the French fleet hence,
And scatter it far and wide,
Or sink it in the sea;
We should be satisfied,
And Thine the Glory be."

This was the prayer I made,
For my soul was all on flame,
And even as I prayed
The answering tempest came;
It came with a mighty power,
Shaking the windows and walls,
And tolling the bell in the tower
As it tolls at funerals.

The lightning suddenly
Unsheathed its flaming sword,
And I cried: "Stand still, and see
The salvation of the Lord!"
The heavens were black with cloud,
The sea was white with hail,
And ever more fierce and loud
Blew the October gale.

The fleet it overtook,
And the broad sails in the van
Like the tents of Cushan shook,
Or the curtains of Midian.
Down on the reeling decks
Crashed the overwhelming seas;
Ah, never were there wrecks
So pitiful as these!

Like a potter's vessel broke
The great ships of the line;
They were carried away as a smoke,
Or sank like lead in the brine.
O Lord! Before Thy path
They vanished and ceased to be,
When Thou didst walk in wrath
With Thine horses through the sea.[6]

The Colonists said victory over the French Fleet was just as great a deliverance as when Moses led Israel out of Egypt through the Red Sea.

When President George Washington referred to *the Invisible Hand which conducts the affairs of men,* could it be that he thought of his own deliverance during the French and Indian Wars [1754-1763]. At that time the Colonies were under British protection, but the French attempted to take the American Colonies away from England. The French badgered the Indians into frequent attacks on Colonists. In 1755, when George Washington was a 23-year-old Lieutenant in the British army, two horses were shot out from under him and four rifle bullets passed through his coat at the Battle of the Monongahela. Of the 1900 British comrades, 1400 were killed. He himself identified the Hand of God as providentially sparing his life. Washington was protected because God had a future role for him in shaping and leading America.

Following the battle, Washington wrote to his brother John, saying: **"But by the all-powerful dispensations of Providence, I have been protected beyond all human probability or expectation; for I had four bullets through my coat, and two horses shot under me, yet escaped unhurt, although death was leveling my companions on every side of me!"[7]**

Fifteen years later a respected Indian Chief came with an interpreter to visit George Washington. Speaking of the Monongahela battle through an interpreter, the chief said: **"I am a chief and ruler over my tribes. I have traveled a long and weary path that I might see the young warrior of the great battle. It was on the day when the white man's blood mixed with the streams of our forests that I first beheld this chief [Washington]. I called to my young men and said, mark yon tall and daring warrior? He is not of the red-coat tribe – he hath an Indian's wisdom, and his warriors fight as we do – himself alone exposed. Quick, let your aim be certain, and he dies. Our rifles were leveled, rifles which knew not how to miss – 'twas all in vain, a power mightier far than we, shielded you. Seeing you were under the special guardianship of the Great Spirit, we immediately ceased to fire** at you . . . Something bids me speak in the voice of prophecy: Listen! The Great Spirit protects that man [pointing at Washington], and guides his destinies – he will become the chief of nations, and a people yet unborn will hail him as the founder of a mighty empire. I am come to pay homage to the man who is the particular favorite of Heaven, and who can never die in battle. I had seventeen fair fires at him with my rifle, and . . . could not bring him to the ground."[8] That is Providence!

Was Washington thinking of the recently concluded Constitutional Convention when, having reached an impasse in the discussion, the oldest delegate, 77-year-old Benjamin Franklin, appealed to the others for prayer. He said, **"I have lived, Sir, a long time, and the longer I live, the more convincing proofs I see of this truth: 'that God governs in the affairs of man.' And if a sparrow cannot fall to the ground without His notice, is it probable that an empire can rise without His aid? I therefore . . . move that, henceforth, prayers imploring the assistance of Heaven and its blessing on our deliberation be held in this assemble every morning before we proceed to business."'[9]** Franklin's appeal marked the turning point. Progress in their discussions grew, for the atmosphere was changed – by the Hand of Divine Providence.

It was the opinion of George Washington and the other Colonists that, while men plan and design as close to an ideal Constitution as possible, it is God who has the final say in its success or failure. This was the restful opinion of the fifty-six men who signed the Declaration of Independence in 1776; they stated in that Declaration that they had "a firm reliance on divine Providence." And because of their firm reliance, that Document became the Foundation, the Backbone, through which life flowed to every Colony and ultimately to every member of North America's civil community.

2 – EDUCATION IN COLONIAL AMERICA

Education in Early America was designed to make one both wise and virtuous. For that to happen, the role of Education was primarily in the hands of the Family and the Church: The role of Government was minimal. Even Thomas Jefferson, not known for his spiritual bent, warned: **"If it is believed that these elementary schools will be better managed by . . . general authority of the government, than by parents within each ward, it is a belief against all experience."**[10] It was not that Government was cold toward Education; the Founders believed education to be vital. For this reason every Township, which consisted of 36 square miles of land, was required to set aside a portion of land for a school. Beyond that, government had no direct hand in the educating process; that was left to the Family and the Church.

Government had no problem with the Church's role in Education. There was no Department of Education, no lobbyists and no governmental funding of teachers or the school administration. In fact, there was little school administration, for that duty was handled by local parents. One of the parents volunteered or was selected to teach, or the parents hired a teacher – or the pastor taught. In any case, families were directly involved in the education of their own children.

Education was vital in early America. Abraham Lincoln said: **"The philosophy of the school room in one generation will be the philosophy of**

government in the next."[11] George Washington said the future of this nation depends on the Christian training of the youth, and furthermore, that it is not possible to govern without the Bible!

The link between education and the Bible in Colonial America is well documented. It was John Quincy Adams who said education was to make one **wise and virtuous.** For that to happen, educators believed Scripture was vital. Our Forefathers resisted sending their youth overseas for their Education because of the deterioration of European education where the French had introduced the goddess of Reason into European culture as well as education. Therefore, schools for the training of Colonial youth were started early: Within sixteen years of Mayflower's landing in 1620, Harvard was founded.

As for the desire that students would be both wise and virtuous, the following remarks from Harvard's 1646 Rules and Precepts give us insight: **"Every one shall consider the main end of his life and studies to know God and Jesus Christ, which is eternal life. "Everyone shall so exercise himself in reading the Scriptures twice a day that they be ready to give an account of their proficiency therein, both in theoretical observations of languages and logic, and in practical and spiritual truths.**[12] Following Harvard, other colleges were founded: Yale [1701]; Princeton [1746]; Dartmouth [1754]; Columbia, Brown and others followed. In fact, **not one** college started before the American Revolution was secular; all were founded by Christians for Christian purposes.

Early Americans knew that a society does not become civil apart from Christianity. Noah Webster defined **"civil"** and **"savage"** as opposites. Man was either Christian [civil] or Savage [uncivilized]. And Webster's wisdom was standard fair in the schools of that day.

Several of the American Founders had been students at Columbia [formerly King's College], founded in 1754. Forrest McDonald, professor of history at the University of Alabama, tells us that in order to enter Columbia, a student in Colonial America was required to **"translate the first ten chapters of the Gospel of John from Greek into Latin, as well as to be expert in arithmetic and to have a blameless moral character."** [Recall that students in early America entered college at fourteen or fifteen years of age.] McDonald then stingingly asks, **how many Americans today could even get into college, given those requirements.**[13]

A graduate from college was equally qualified to enter three professions: teaching, preaching or law.

When Noah Webster was seventy years old in 1828, he published his ***Dictionary of the English Language***. By that time he had mastered twenty-five languages. It is wisdom on our part to defer to Webster's grasp of Education. He said, **"Education comprehends all that series of instruction and discipline which is intended to enlighten the understanding, correct the temper, and form the manners and habits of youth, and fit them for usefulness in their future stations. To give children a good education in manners, arts and science,** is important; to give them a religious education is indispensable; and an immense responsibility rests on parents and guardians who neglect these duties."[14]

Early documents verify the fact that Churches were the primary instrumentality for the education of youth. The Northwest Ordinance, adopted in 1787 shortly before our present Constitution, had provisional control over the territory that included the present states of Ohio, Indiana, Illinois, Michigan, Wisconsin, and part of Minnesota before that territory was divided into states. Article III of the Ordinance states: **"Religion, morality, and knowledge, being necessary to good government and the happiness of mankind, schools and the means of education shall forever be encouraged."**[15] Here we see the link between religion and schools.

Three years later George Washington, in his first Annual Address to Congress, said, **"Knowledge is in every country the surest basis of public happiness. Whether this desirable object will be best promoted by affording aids to seminaries of learning already established, by the institution of a national university, or by any other expedients will be well worthy of a place in the deliberations of the Legislature."**[16] Neither today's media nor the ACLU would take kindly to a President's suggestion that the House and Senate consider aid to seminaries. They would not think kindly of Thomas Jefferson who, throughout his eight-year term of office, went to the House of Representatives every Sunday morning where the largest church service in America was held. Nor would they approve using the U.S. Supreme Court chambers for Christian meetings, but it happened!

To further validate the Bible's primary place in the minds of early Americans, consider a letter sent by John Quincy Adams [1767-1848], our sixth President, to his young son who was away at school. He encouraged him to follow "dad's" example, saying: **"I have myself, for many years, made it a practice to read through the Bible once every year . . . and you should also do so for the purpose of making you wiser and more virtuous."**[17]

Adams recognized the validity of Martin Luther's warning in the 16th Century: **"I am much afraid that schools will prove to be great gates of hell unless they diligently labor in explaining the Holy Scriptures, engraving them in the hearts of youth. I advise no one to place his child where the Scriptures do not reign paramount. Every institution in which men are not increasingly occupied with the Word of God must become corrupt."**[18]

Three things are obvious: [1] Virtue and happiness are inseparable! [2] Biblical education tends to make men virtuous! [3] Those that are Biblically educated are happy indeed! So, our Founders understood the remark in the Declaration of Independence regarding *"the pursuit of happiness"* did not pertain to everyone having a right to do their own thing, but with finding fulfillment and happiness as a useful and productive member of society.

George Washington linked morality and religion, concluding his Presidential career by saying, **"And let us with caution indulge the supposition that morality can be maintained without religion . . . reason and experience both forbid us to expect that national morality can prevail in exclusions of religious principle."**[19]

Noah Webster said that **". . . the principles of republican government have their origin in the Scriptures."** He added: **"In my view, the Christian religion is the most important and one of the first things in which all children, under a free government, ought to be instructed . . . No truth is more evident to my mind than that the Christian religion must be the basis of any government intended to secure the rights and privileges of a free people. . . . When I speak of the Christian religion as the basis of government, I do not mean an ecclesiastical establishment, a creed, or rites, forms, and ceremonies, or any compulsion of conscience. I mean primitive Christianity in its simplicity as taught by Christ and His apostles, consisting in a belief in the being, perfections, and moral government of God; in the revelation of His will to men, as their supreme rule of action; in man's accountability to God for his conduct in this life; and in the indispensable obligation of all men to yield entire obedience to God's commands in the moral law and in the Gospel."**[20]

It is close to impossible for us in the 21st Century to appreciate the wisdom that flowed from Colonial institutions of education. All of them were founded, not to grant degrees but to make students wise and virtuous and fit them for usefulness in their future stations. Their education produced men of character. Even those who had not attended college were readers: There were more newspapers in the Colonies than in France. Professor McDonald, mentioned earlier, read virtually every publication written in the Colonies from their beginnings to the Convention in 1787. He was convinced it would have been easy in America in 1787 to have assembled another five, possibly ten, constitutional conventions that would have matched the actual convention in every way except, of course, for the incomparable luster of George Washington.

In its initial stages, the Constitution was not designed to control the lives of citizens. John Adams, in an address to the military in 1798, said our Constitution was made for a moral and religious people, and that it was **"wholly inadequate for the government of any other."**[21] Men were to be self-governing: It was the role of Christian education to develop self-government in the student. Only a tyrannical king could arbitrarily govern the ungoverned. Education in Colonial America was for all practical purposes, Christian Education!

Education and Christianity are inseparable. When God created Man He installed in him the Law of Nature. [Note: The Law of Nature, or Natural Law, consists of those principles installed by God in nature at the time of Creation. The Law of Nature is evident in the automatic growth process of animals and plant life, and also in the instincts of animals, i.e., a lion attacking a deer, or birds flying south at the appropriate time. The Law of Nature also includes Inalienable Rights and Freedoms God gave to man at the time of Creation.] Education takes into account the nature of the student: This is in keeping with the Law of Nature. Christianity too takes into account the nature of the student. More later!

While modern education attempts to develop the innate capacities of the student, Noah Webster believed that the teacher had something to impart to the student: This is evident from the words Webster uses, such as **instruction, discipline, enlighten, correct** and **inform**. No grade school or high school student – or college student for that matter – has the innate ability to develop character on his own. Left to himself he will develop a self-centered mentality, a gang mindset, much like the beasts of earth. Such is the extent of innate goodness! Webster's definition makes it apparent that the teacher is a person of sterling character. Only a godly teacher has something to impart to students. To have the qualities of a good teacher, he or she must first be disciplined and enlighten after a godly sort – and have the compassion and wisdom to impart all vital character traits and essentials to the student.

3 – RIGHTS IN COLONIAL AMERICA

The Declaration of Independence reads: **"We hold these truths to be self-evident, that all men are created equal, that they are endowed by their Creator with certain unalienable Rights, that among these are Life, Liberty and the pursuit of Happiness."**

The Colonists believed that **"pursuit of Happiness"** meant Property: That is, a man was happiest when living in peace and safety on his own Property. The Founders drew this picture from 1 Kings 4:25 where it is said that *"Judah and Israel lived in safety, every man under his own vine and fig tree."* That, to the Founders, was Happiness! It is the political philosopher, John Locke [1632-1704], who reveals this **"pursuit of Happiness"** concept. And it is John Locke's writings that inspired Thomas Jefferson concepts for the Declaration of Independence.

John Locke and our Founders understood that Rights came from God and were Inalienable. [Note: The word Unalienable carries the same meaning as our current Inalienable.] An Inalienable Right cannot be separated from the person who received it. God alone has the authority to remove a Right He granted. Even the one who possesses a Right has no authority to give it away. Government however can remove a Right, but only under God's directive – as in the case where a murderer's life is to be forfeited for the life he murdered [Numbers 35:16-18].

Samuel Adams [1722-1803], President John Adams' cousin, was deeply concerned that Colonists would willingly give up certain rights in order to live peaceably with others. Adams said it is a great absurdity to sacrifice essential rights as a means of preserving other rights, adding, **"If men, through fear, fraud, or mistake, should in terms renounce or give up any essential natural right, the eternal law of reason and the grand end of society would absolutely vacate such renunciation. The right to freedom being the gift of God Almighty, it is not in the power of man to alienate this gift and voluntarily become a slave."[22]**

Samuel Adams identified the purpose for Government, saying the grand end of civil government is for the support, protection, and defence of man's rights. We dare NOT forget that Rights are from God and therefore, are to be held in trust for Him Who gave them, to be returned to Him at the end of life. Even national defense relates to the citizens' Rights. That is the reason why America defends her borders – to protect every citizen's Life, Liberty and Property. There need be no other reason for national defense.

Monarchs of earlier days – whether willingly or blindly – were unfamiliar with the inalienable Rights of citizens. It was taken for granted by ruler and ruled alike that kings could – under the tyrannical theory of the Divine Right of Kings – regulate and control all citizens. The American Founders designed our government in such a way that it left the citizen free to be self-governed. To be self-governed a man had to be free. In fact, for a citizen to be considered a

Freeman he had to own property and not be dependent on any other: Property in this case meant real estate, or simply coins in the pocket. For this reason, only Freemen voted. After all, if a man was beholden to another he would be tempted to vote to place a portion of the other citizen's property into his own sack. In the final analysis Freeman ran the affairs of state. This, however, encouraged those without property into being frugal and energetic so that they too could partake in the voting process.

Today, due to selfishness and the abundance of law-suits – supposed rights of all types are added to our laws: criminal rights, gay rights, women's rights, children's rights, black's rights, renters' rights, minority rights, etc., etc., etc. Courts have failed to understand or embrace the Constitutional idea of inalienable rights. Or is it that citizens have failed to understand their inalienable rights and claim them. Our Founders understood that Rights came from the Creator, not from government. And because of its origin, it was considered a religious right, not to be messed with by government or neighbor. Government existed to protect Rights granted by God. And above all, Government was certainly not empowered to add rights to certain classes of citizens. How foolish to think that man could add rights to the ones permanently installed by God! Even Thomas Jefferson, the Deist, understood, saying that **our right to life, liberty, the use of our faculties, the pursuit of happiness, are impressed upon the sense of every man. We do not claim these under the charters of kings or**

legislators, but under the King of kings.[23] Amazing – and wonderfully true!

This brings us to a critical question: Does the pornographer have a **right** to spread his immoral influence? Does the scandal magazine have a **right** to libel anyone? Does the **right** to **"happiness"** include drunkenness, marijuana and suicide? Society needs constitutional answers to these questions. If not, Americans will be in constant pursuit of more and more wrongs and call them rights. This will be so because of two errant ideas: [1] that government has an endless storehouse of rights it can grant to citizens at will; and [2] that government was installed to secure the privacy of citizens so they may do whatever the flesh demands. And the flesh – being the flesh – will always demand more and more.

Freedom of Speech

Our Forefathers understood that Freedom of Speech came from God the Creator. He who gave the ability to speak gave the Freedom to speak. Our Founders understood this! They also understood that the Freedom to speak did not include the Freedom to slander another. Forrest McDonald of the University of Alabama points out that in Colonial America libel was not legal, even if true. It was lawful to speak disparagingly of the reputation of another, **"because, whether true or false, it was equally dangerous to the public peace."**[24]

The Christian has an added injunction – to be *"speaking the truth in love,"* for it is only the truth that brings a person to the place of growing up in Christ. [Eph.4:15] The motive for a Christian to exercise his guaranteed Freedom of Speech is not to relieve himself by pouring out his opinion on every topic. Freedom to open the mouth is not the same as the Freedom to speak the truth. Paul tells the Ephesians that *"no unwholesome word should proceed from your mouth, but only such a word as will enlighten and improve your hearer according to the need of the moment—that the spoken words may give grace to those who hear."* [Eph.4:29] Blessed indeed is the man who is *"quick to hear and slow to speak."* [James 1:19] When that is the case, not only is the speaker blessed, everyone who listens is blessed as well.

Freedom of Worship

We further ask: Why did God grant, and the Bill of Rights guarantee, the Inalienable Right to worship?

Every right given is rooted in a duty! Because man has the **duty** to worship God he was granted the **right** to do so. It is because of this **right** to worship God that men and women for 2,000 years have been willing to die rather than give up that **right**. Because that **right** came from God, it is Inalienable and therefore protected by the Constitution. On the other hand, an atheist does not have a God-given right to reject God or espouse atheism. Nor does the Christian have the right to force Christianity upon a world that is unwilling to listen. Consider the difference between Freedoms and Rights: A man is free to be an atheist but that is not a Right. Nor does a man have a Right to be a Moslem or a Pagan: He has freedom to rebel against the true God and be whatever he chooses, but cannot claim that God Himself gave him that Right. It is true that God gave every man Freedom – even Freedom to destroy himself – but he has no such Right. A wrong can never be converted to being a right!

Because of the unbreakable link between **rights** and **duties**, the church and school in Colonial days educated listeners to appreciate their **rights** and embrace their **duties**. Here we see the union between the church and the school, as well as the union between **education** and **rights**.

Consider the **Inalienability** of the Right to Worship! Inasmuch as Government did not grant that Right, it cannot remove it. For that matter, neither can Government take that Right away if it is not used. It simply lies dormant until such time as the citizen exercises his God-given Right to worship. Should the time come when Moslem's Shariah law is enforced here in America [which is already taking place in European countries], they may take away our Freedoms, but can never remove our Rights. It may cost us our lives but, in the process, we do not lose our *"right to the tree of life"* [Revelation 22:14] nor our *"right to be a child of God."* [John 1:12]

At times in the past believers attempted to force Christianity on society. This was so during the days of the Holy Roman Empire when everyone within the borders of the empire was considered a Christian and under certain religious obligations. John Calvin also enforced his brand of Christianity on Geneva, Switzerland: Nuns had to convert or be banned from the city. Enforcement was neither the ministry of Jesus nor the assigned duty of the Church. Her function is to preach the message of redemption and forgiveness through Jesus Christ. She is to bring people to faith in Jesus Christ, and that can only be done in Freedom. She is to do this even when the State opposes those who are loyal to Christ.

A wrong can never be a right! That which injures another is a wrong and cannot be a right even though approved by legislators or sanctioned by courts. This is glaringly true in the abortion industry. The wrong treatment of the unborn cannot be considered a Right – for a wrong cannot be a right, though demanded in China or sanctioned in Chicago. Abortion – more accurately termed aborticide, the intentional destruction of a child in the womb, is a violation of natural law inasmuch as it is a violation of the Right to Life of the unborn child.

Defining Inalienable Rights

To determine the legitimacy of any claimed right, we ask: What is the **duty** from which that specific **right** originated?

A man has the right to marry because of the Biblical duty to replenish the earth. But what is the Biblical duty of the homosexual?

On this same basis, does a man have a right to be drunk in his own residence, a right to recklessly drive his car on an abandoned highway, or a right to grow marijuana on his private property for personal use? What about the right to commit suicide? In each case a man may exercise the Freedom to selfishly pursue his own interests but, again, a wrong can never become a Right.

This does not mean that government has an automatic right to invade a private home. But it does mean there is **NO Biblical duty** to be drunk, to drive recklessly, to use marijuana, or to commit suicide? Again we ask: From which **spiritual duty** does that **right** originate?

It is clear that George Washington understood duties as evidenced in his announcement of the first National Thanksgiving Day, saying: **"Whereas it is the duty of all nations to acknowledge the providence of Almighty God, to obey His will, to be grateful for His benefits, and humbly to implore His protection and favor . . . I do recommend and assign Thursday, the 26th day of November next . . . that we may then all unite in rendering unto Him our sincere and humble thanks for His kind care and protection . . ."**[25] It is obvious here that Washington also understood Providence!

He also knew that government was not authorized by God to enforce Christian worship. But it was the duty of government to provide opportunity for citizen's to fulfill their God-ordained duty. With this in mind Congress sanctioned the printing of Bibles for use in the conversion of the Indians as well as for use in schools. A non-coercive atmosphere allows some to move away from God; others to move toward Him.

The Christian's attitude regarding Jesus Christ's relationship to the culture needs to be re-evaluated. The liberal has fairly well eliminated Jesus from the public square and the classroom. The Christian conservative, having both charity and a weak backbone, bows before the law of man. So the liberal teaches evolution and secular humanism unchecked and without a serious challenge, despite the fact that the Bible-believer has the truth on his side. It has now reached the stage where the Biblical worldview is no longer allowed alongside of the pagan worldview in the classroom. A 2008 film documentary by Ben Stein, entitled **_Expelled_**, revealed that university and college professors can often be fired if they even want to discuss intelligent design in their classroom. The whole educational structure is controlled by the evolutionist, the naturalist, the secular humanist. No longer are students allowed to openly debate or even discuss the possibility of creationism. While the Bible-believer yields his position ever so kindly, the liberal is not so generous: The door of his mind is solidly closed to all other views but his own. Furthermore, he is convinced that the Bible-believer who would allow the teaching of both — Creationism and Evolution — must not be too convinced on what he believes. And the firm Christian, while he knows evolution to be the foolish notion of natural man, allows the liberal the freedom to destroy himself. I suppose the Christian is right in this – for God Himself allows the liberal that freedom.

The political liberal and the religious liberal agree: They both desire to belittle and remove the Biblical record of Jesus from society. Both would be well pleased had Jesus never lived. In order to expunge the record of Jesus Christ from American culture it is necessary to get the U.S. Courts to approve the erecting of a fictitious wall of separation between church and state. The phrase, **"building a wall of separation between Church and State,"** is found in a letter written by President Thomas Jefferson to the Danbury Baptists who were concerned that government would interfere with their freedoms. Jefferson assured them as follows: **"Believing with you that religion is a matter which lies solely between man and his God, that he owes account to none other for faith or his worship . . . that act of the whole American people . . . declared that their legislature should 'make no law respecting an establishment of religion, or prohibiting the free exercise thereof, thus <u>building a wall of separation between Church and State</u>."**[26] Simply put, the Baptists who were a bit wary of Jefferson due to his Deistic views[27] were now assured by him that the State has no authority to interfere in Church matters. The Church rightly had input into government, but no control. On the other hand, government has neither input nor control of the Church. Church members, yes, if they should commit a crime!

In Everson v Board of Education, Justice Black of the U.S. Supreme Court inserted the **"wall of separation"** idea [referred to as the Establishment Clause] into the case and it has become immovably trapped in our culture and our laws. It has been used to silence the opinions of Christians in the schools and in the public arena, something Jefferson never intended.

Rights are not merely a good idea. Nor are they granted to man by social arrangement or agreement. It is not a communal tradeoff between Government and the citizen, that is: I'll let you do certain thing if you let me do certain things. Inalienable Rights did not come from the King of England, from Government, or even from America's Founders. Rights were given to Man by God Himself. For that matter, Government has no relationship to Rights, except that it is the Government's duty to see that the citizen's Rights are protected. Government does not exist to expand its own sphere of power or authority, but is instituted by God to defend each citizen's Inalienable Rights. Furthermore, each citizen is to be as concerned with the Rights of his neighbor as he is with his own: In this way he fulfills God's command to love his neighbor as he loves himself [Luke 10:27; Romans 13:8].

4 – LAW IN COLONIAL AMERICA

One day a young man told me he was an atheist. I said: **"You're not old enough to be an atheist."** He was about twenty-five. A couple days later I saw him again and asked, **"Do you know why God gave the Ten Commandments?"** After a light-hearted quip he admitted he did not know. I said, **"So I don't kill you!"** It took about a half-second for him to broadly smile as he realized what a wonderful world it would be without murder, adultery or theft.

God loves the Law, its inherent simplicity and its benefits for both God and man. We too would love the Law if we could just get it right! The Law of God is good for us! Moses wrote that God's Law was given to us so **"that it may go well"** with us. (See Deuteronomy 4:40; 5:16; 5:29; 6:3; 6:18; 12:25; 22:7) The simpler the laws the happier are those who live under them. When the Colonies broke from Great Britain they had no laws. John Locke [1632-1704] called this the **"state of nature."** The Colonies had to start from scratch. What would America look like: The color of American law would be the color of America! It was an act of Providence that men were raised up for such a time as this, men who knew where to search to find solid answers to their quest for wisdom. Here were men who knew what to do, and how to do it!

In this chapter we want to show how Law developed in America, how it functioned, and how – like an aged patient – it declined into our present judicial condition.

The first permanent written law in America was the Mayflower Compact. By the Providence of God the Pilgrims found their way from the Old World to the New. They landed in Massachusetts, not Virginia where the British Crown had authorized the planting of a Colony. Having been blown off course by the winds of God, they were under the authority of no one: They were on their own! So they created their own law before they disembarked from the ship: They drew up the Mayflower Compact. The signers of this compact agreed to **"covenant and combine ourselves together into a civil Body Politic."** Lest they become scattered when they went ashore, the compact contained a promise that, whatever just and equal laws they would pass – they agreed to give those laws **"all due Submission and Obedience."** In this way the Mayflower Compact made them one political entity, one nation, one civil body. Though they acknowledged the Crown in the compact, they were really on their own. The Pilgrims came to be free from religious persecution and oppressive taxation. Here they could teach their children to know God. The dead dry bones, a mere religious skeleton of the past, could once again experience the breath of God and live.

Written law is required in a civil society: But how did this come about in America. By what authority could a Declaration of Independence be written? What were the laws of Great Britain that could allow such a shameful act – shameful at least to the British! In the Old World, law was whatever the king said it was. Perhaps this is where Chief Justice Charles

Evans Hughes [1862-1948] of the U.S. Supreme Court got his idea that: **"The Constitution is what the judges say it is."**[26] He simply replaced the British king with the Supreme Court as the entity with the final word.

As time went on, the Crown acted arbitrarily against the Colonies, increasing taxation, restricting worship, housing soldiers in Colonial homes, even passing the Stamp Act which required a fee on every piece of paper printed in America, as well as other oppressive measures. The Colonists longed to break free from British controls. But being law abiding folks, many of whom had been deeply affected by the Great Spiritual Awakening a few years earlier, they could not arbitrarily declare themselves at Liberty from Britain: Such a major step must be legal.

In 1761, Massachusetts lawyer James Otis drew upon an ancient idea in law, the idea of Natural Law. He introduced it into a court case and, though he lost, other Colonies picked up on it and began to employ Natural Law: It simply said that if an Act of Parliament was against any of God's Natural Laws, the Act of Parliament would be void, being contrary to eternal truth, equity and justice. Through this process more and more Colonists were realizing that there was a Law that took priority over the British Crown. This truth was further bolstered by the Great Awakening. It certainly seemed like the dry bones were coming together, and the breath of God was infusing those once dead bones with life.

Parliament was getting frustrated with Colonial leanings toward independence. In 1766 it passed the Declaratory Act which said that Parliament had full power and authority to make laws and statutes of sufficient force and validity to bind the colonies and people of America to the British Crown in all cases whatsoever. Parliament believed the Colonies very existence rested solely with the British Crown.[28] When the American Colonies sought relief from oppression – oppression increased!

Along came John Dickerson who wrote an unsigned series of newspaper articles entitled ***Letters from a Farmer in Pennsylvania***. In this persuasive series he impressed his many readers with the fact that there was an unwritten English Constitution which acts of Parliament were violating. Even Britain's Sir Edward Coke, sixty years earlier, had ruled that whenever Parliament passed an act contrary to the unwritten Constitution, the common law prevails and voids the act. Coke's view had faded from usage by the time the Colonists needed it: The law at that time was whatever Parliament said it was, regardless of the unwritten Constitution or Common Law. It was well understood that England had authority to control citizens on her own shores; but did she have authority to control colonists on American shores?

Due to the many oppressive measures against the colonies, one option remained: Appeal to the Crown for help! In 1774 the First Continental Congress sent a petition to the Crown asking for a redress of grievances. King George III ignored it: Troops had already been sent to suppress any American resistance. The Colonists found another option: It was in John Locke's ***Two Treatises of***

Civil Government! Locke had maintained that in the distant past man existed in a state of nature without government. In this state man had God-given Rights to life, liberty and property! Because man is sinful, Locke contended, he forms governments to defend individuals in the enjoyment of their natural rights. As long as government performed its duties in this regard it was to be obeyed; if not it was the right of the people to form a new government that would properly function. On this basis – the basis of Natural Law – the Colonies found their freedom to declare independence from Britain. They realized, however, if this venture into independence was to be a success it could only take place under the Hand of Providence. And so they wrote into the Document – **"for the support of this Declaration, with a firm reliance on the protection of Divine Providence, we mutually pledge to each other our Lives, our Fortunes, and our sacred Honor."** The rest is history! These bones, once dead and dry, scattered across the landscape of Europe, had come to life on American shores. No Englishman in the 1600s could have ever imagined the life and liberty Colonial Americans would enjoy.

Now that Americans were free from British control, how would they formulate law? At the center of their consideration was this: God, being the source of all valid law, He should never be offended! That being settled in their hearts, they also acknowledged that God was the author of two types of law: The Law of Nature written in the hearts of all men regarding right and wrong; and the Revealed Law of God found in Christian Scriptures. Prior to the Declaration of Independence, the Crown not only stood in the way of the Colonies in their desire to obey the Law of Nature and the Revealed Law, the Crown itself did not obey those laws. The writings of men like Locke, Puffendorf, Grotius and Samuel Rutherford [1600-1661] greatly influenced Colonial thinking. Rutherford's ***Lex Rex*** [The Law and the Prince] was based on the premise that the king who disobeys God's Law un-kings himself. As the king of England continued to violate Colonial Rights, respect for him continued to diminish.

It is God who authorized the proper use of Law – as Peter tells us – that government exists *"for the punishment of evil-doers, and the praise of the one who does well."* [1 Peter 2:14] Now that is simple enough: If a man lived in isolation – as in a state of nature – he would be his own government. However, living as he does in society with others, a person or persons are elected or anointed by God to see that laws are obeyed: This is called Government!

During the deliberations that brought about both the Declaration of Independence and the U.S. Constitution, the French Enlightenment attempted to influence the delegates. Because the Enlightenment excluded God, however, it never made much headway. In fact, Forrest McDonald states: **"Americans were all but untouched by the writers of the French Enlightenment. . . Americans were immune to the antireligious virus that had infected the French. Instead, all public men could be expected to be versed in a half-dozen general categories of writings in addition, of course, to the Holy**

Bible. They cited the Bible more than any other source, and unsurprisingly, the most cited Book of the Bible was Deuteronomy." [29] It is worth noting that Christians like President John Adams strongly resisted Thomas Paine, the French deist. Abigail Adams, John's wife, spoke out forcefully against Paine who desired revolution in order to destroy law. John Adams and his wife Abigail wanted revolution to establish law. Paine sought anarchy: Adams sought order.

James Madison said that Sir William Blackstone's ***Commentaries on the Laws of England*** was **"in every man's hand."** Perhaps that stretched the truth a bit. However, more copies of Blackstone were sold in America than there were lawyers. That meant that farmers and merchants were reading Blackstone, which was **"the second most frequently cited author in all the American political literature from the 1760s through the 1780s."** [30] Deuteronomy and Blackstone embodied the basic principles upon which our Republic was formed.

Blackstone's insight into the Law of Nature is priceless. He writes: **"Man, considered as a creature, must necessarily be subject to the laws of his Creator, for he is entirely a dependent being. . . As man depends absolutely upon his Maker for everything, it is necessary that he should in all points conform to his Maker's will. This will of his Maker is called the law of nature."** Blackstone continues: **"This law of nature, being coeval** [that is, contemporary - ed.] **with mankind and dictated by God Himself, is of course superior in obligation** to any other. It is binding over all the globe in all countries, and at all times: no human laws are of any validity, if contrary to this; and such of them as are valid derive all their force, and all their authority. . . from this original."[31]

John Locke [1632-1704] had a major influence on America. Thomas Jefferson [1743-1826] carried Locke's ideas on into the Declaration of Independence. Locke said **"the Law of Nature stands as an eternal rule to all men, legislators as well as others. The rules they make . . . must be conformable to the Law of Nature, i.e. to the will of God. . . Laws human must be made according to the general laws of Nature, and without contradiction to any positive law of Scripture, otherwise they are ill made."[32]**

Because the Founders studied Locke and Blackstone and Deuteronomy they were aware that the Law of Nature was timeless; it was a Law not to be abused or ignored. It had continual effects on the culture of that day and beyond. It was not merely an imaginary concept invented by man or developed in anarchy. The Law of Nature was fixed in man's world by God Himself and is designed to govern all of his relations.

The writings of Blackstone had an ongoing effect: Evangelist Charles G. Finney was born almost 70 years after Blackstone, but was greatly affected by him. We do not know all that prompted this young lawyer in the early-1800s to open his Bible and seek God. But there is no doubt that Finney was greatly encouraged in that direction by reading Blackstone's

__Commentaries__, which every law office contained. Finney sounded very much like Blackstone when he wrote in his __Systematic Theology:__ ...**no government is lawful or innocent that does not recognize the moral law as the only universal law, and God as the Supreme Lawgiver and Judge, to whom nations in their national capacity, as well as individuals, are amenable. God puts forth no enactments, but such as are declaratory of the Common Law of the Universe . . . All legislation, not recognizing the Moral Law as the only Law of the Universe, are null and void, and all attempts to establish and enforce them are odious tyranny and usurpation.**[33] That would have made Blackstone proud!

The Law of Nature was given by God, and was therefore superior to legislator and judge. It was neither the legislator's role nor the judge's prerogative to create law: They were to apply the Law of Nature to the American legal scene. The Founders' over-arching desire was to formulate their laws so as not to offend God, for they recognized Him as the Original and only true Lawgiver [See Isaiah 33:22; James 4:12].

In 1789 the French __Declaration of the Rights of Man__ was based solely on man's desire for self-realization with no reference to the person or will of God. The French __Declaration__ has its roots in the serpent's deception in the Garden of Eden when he said: *"You shall be your own god, knowing good and evil."* [Gen.3:5] The American __Declaration__ is based on the knowledge of God, the Founders having come to know God through Jesus Christ. The French had

Adam and Eve as their source of wisdom; America's Founders had God and His Son Jesus Christ.

There are three possible sources for Law: People, Rulers or God. The American Founders chose God as their source of Law – and the greatest nation ever to rise on the earth was the convincing evidence that there is indeed a Hand of Providence in the affairs of men. The Founders get the credit for knowing what God was looking for – but God alone deserves the praise and glory for overseeing this new experiment with His Hand of Providence.

To understand Constitutional law we start with Common Law, which is based on the Moral Law of God. It is also related to the common sense of godly men of good conscience. On the other hand, Equity Law, which is now used in our court system, relies on case law as well as the opinion of judges who can apply convoluted reasoning in arriving at their rulings. An ACLU lawyer, for example, can usually find case law that justifies putting down Christian expression. No one can correct the court's finding because it was determined by means of the legal process in Equity law. This would not happen under Common Law, but often occurs in Equity. God can be readily excluded from the Equity courtroom but cannot be barred from Common Law, for He is its very Foundation. Without Him there is no Common Law or Moral Law.

As for Blackstone, present-day attorneys no longer use him; they use various law dictionaries and case findings in their study of law as well as in their cases before the judge. Neither judge nor lawyer uses Blackstone's ***Common Law***. The reason is simple: Equity law has replaced Common law which resides in the consciences of good men. In the meantime, there is no room in Equity for the following truth addressed to us by Blackstone: **"The doctrines thus delivered we call the revealed or divine law, and they are to be found only in the Holy Scriptures. . . . We are not from thence to conclude that the knowledge of these truths was attainable by reason, in its present corrupted state; since we find that, until they were revealed, they were hid from the wisdom of ages."** Lest we think that this has nothing to do with justice or law or the court room, Blackstone concludes: **Upon these two foundations, the <u>law of nature</u> and the <u>law of revelation</u>, depend all human laws; that is to say, no human laws should be suffered to contradict these."**[34]

This agrees with the earlier remarks of Finney in which he said that **no government is lawful or innocent that does not recognize the moral law as the only universal law, and God as the Supreme Lawgiver and Judge, to whom nations in their national capacity, as well as individuals, are amenable. God puts forth no enactments, but such as are declaratory of the Common Law of the Universe . . .**

Inasmuch as Common Law has been replaced by Courts of Equity in our current system, was the switchover constitutionally legal? One particular phrase in the Constitution would seem to justify the judiciary as the final arbiter in all cases. That phrase is found in Art.III, Sec.2-1, which reads: **"The judicial Power shall extend to all Cases, in Law and Equity, arising under this Constitution . . ."** From this it has been concluded that the judges have the final word. This was not Thomas Jefferson's understanding: He said that **"there is not a word in the constitution which has given that power to them more than to the executive or legislative branches."** There is further evidence that the Common Law should be our law today. The Northwest Ordinance, passed by Congress on July 13, 1787, was designed to rule over an area from Ohio to Minnesota until that area was divided into states. That Ordinance tells us that within that land area judicial proceedings were to be conducted **"according to the course of the common law"** and Religion **"shall forever be encouraged."**[35] Twelve years later, Thomas Jefferson, referring to the whole nation, said that **"The common law . . . was not in force when we landed here nor till we had formed ourselves into a nation and had manifested by the organs we constituted that <u>the common law was to be our law</u>."** Jefferson then concluded that America **"did not change its former declarations that the common law was its law."**[36] This makes it clear that the Common Law was never to be abandoned in favor of the present Equity system.

5 – CHRISTIANITY IN COLONIAL AMERICA

Philip Schaff tells us, **"In the first three centuries, the Church enjoyed the greatest Liberty by reason of her entire separation from the State."** Once the Church was recognized by the State as a legal entity, the State and the Church became merged as one unit. This process started under Emperor Constantine between 311 and 325. Soon Christianity was installed as the official religion of the Roman Empire. Previously the heathen Empire persecuted Christians; soon the Church/State combo forced the heathen to convert or face persecution. Instead of people being born again by the preaching of the Word, **"by taking in the whole population of the Roman Empire the church became . . . a church of the world. Christianity became a matter of fashion. The number of hypocrites and formal professors rapidly increased . . . heathen customs and usages crept into the worship of God . . ."**[37] During the early 400s the Roman Empire began to collapse and the Christians wondered why. Appealing to Salvian, the Jeremiah of his day, he said: **"Think of your vileness and your crimes, and see whether you are worthy of the divine protection."**[38] After the city of Treves, Germany was almost destroyed by the barbarians, the few surviving "Christian" nobles made a request of the emperor: The first thing they wanted was to re-establish the circus games for entertainment to lift their spirits as a remedy for the ruined city. They desired games rather than seeking the face of God. The atheists saw Christians to be worse than the barbarians, for only the Christians had the Scripture – which they ignored and violated.[39]

Schaff lamented the fact that the Church/State union still had ill effects on the European church in his day [1889]. How unlike the American Church that broke out of European bondage and entanglements with the signing of the Declaration of Independence! Of all the American entities that were benefited in 1776, the greatest blessing came to the Church: She had been forever freed from Spirit-quenching Church/State entanglements. Thomas Jefferson was especially alert in this area, declaring, **"I have sworn upon the altar of God eternal hostility against every form of tyranny over the mind of man."**[40] Jefferson knew history, so he was fully aware of the dangers in a Church/State union. Although the Founders were obedient to God as they framed the Declaration of Independence and Constitution, but it is doubtful they really knew the extent of what they had done.

Proverbs 23:7 tells us, **"As a man thinketh in his heart, so is he!"** What a man thinks about in the deepest nook and crevice of his heart is the most important thing about him. The thoughts of early Americans centered on Rights and Liberty and Justice and Union – but the singular core of those thoughts and desires was Jesus Christ. Their ambition was not merely to secure their Inalienable Rights and Freedoms during their own lifetime, but they desired generations to come to enjoy those same Rights and Freedoms. This was quite unlike King

Hezekiah who, when the prophet Isaiah told him that all his forefathers laid up in store, and even King Hezekiah's own children would go into captivity, said in essence: *"That's a good word: At least I'll have peace during my lifetime!"* [Isa.39:5-8]

Pleasing Jesus Christ was the Central goal of Colonists! All else was secondary, and it was contingent on Jesus Christ maintaining His right place in the personal lives as well as the corporate life of Americans. They knew if His Hand of Providence was absent there was nothing they could do to secure Liberty.

Richard Henry Lee [1732-1794], a signer of the Declaration of Independence, said that experience of all times shows Religion to be the guardian of morals, maintaining that both the happiness of a people and the preservation of civil government depend on piety, religion and morality.

This view was also espoused by George Washington as evidenced in his Farewell Address: **"Of all the dispositions and habits which lead to a political prosperity, religion and morality are indispensable supports. In vain would that man claim the tribute of patriotism, who should labour to subvert these great pillars of human happiness."**[41] In other words, no man is a patriot if he undermines religion and morality; and by religion Washington meant Protestant Christianity!

Observe the explanation of this from Professor Forrest McDonald of the University of Alabama: **"American religion was Protestant, and even those few who professed themselves to be Deists**

. . . shared a Protestant Christian world view. A telling example is seen in the Virginia Bill of Rights of 1776, which declared that 'all men are equally entitled to the free exercise of religion, according to the dictates of their conscience,' but went on to say that 'it is the mutual duty of all to practice Christian forbearance, love, and charity towards each other.' Similarly, the First Congress, which approved the religious-establishment clause of the First Amendment, also appointed a Protestant chaplain."[42]

The essential doctrines of Protestant Christianity in Colonial days might not include elements we would deem essential, but did include this much: [1] Jesus Christ is the Savior of the world; [2] Man is basically sinful and in need of forgiveness; [3] Because of his fallen nature, a man elected to office needs the restriction of a Constitution to keep him from foolishness; [4] Jesus' death paid the penalty for man's sin; and [5] There is a day coming when God will bring all men to judgment. Christianity throughout all time has held to these tenets. Colonial America had one more principle we moderns have forgotten: [6] Jesus Christ was rightful Ruler of the world and by His Hand of Providence was involved in the civil and cultural affairs of this land. He reigns over all and favors those who rely on Him.

The Providence of God oversees individual men; He also engineers the successes and failures of nations. When young George Washington was preparing to go off to military duty, his mother said to him: **"Remember that God only is our sure trust.**

To Him, I commend you. My son, neglect not the duty of secret prayer." There is evidence he followed his mother's counsel. Each morning he rose at 4:00 a.m., for prayer and Bible reading, doing this aloud for an hour in a private room. Each evening from 9:00 to 10:00 p.m., he did the same regardless of the guests in his home. They often overheard him read and pray in a distant room. This practice continued even after he became President of the United States, and only on rare occasions did **"official"** business keep him from his private appointments with God.

As a young lad Washington prayed, **"Let my heart, therefore, gracious God, be so affected with the glory and majesty of (Thine honor) that I may not do mine own works, but wait on Thee, and discharge those weighty duties which Thou requires of me . . . Wash away my sins in the immaculate Blood of the Lamb . . . Daily frame me more and more into the likeness of Thy Son Jesus Christ . . . Thou gavest Thy Son to die for me; and hast given me assurance of salvation . . ."**[43]

The Christianity of our Founders seemed more alive than today's brand which is becoming more and more commonplace with time. Their relationship with God was vital. Above all else, they were careful never to offend Him. Their Christianity was not stuck in Church on Monday morning: It was an essential aspect of their daily lives. John Jay, as we know, was the first Chief Justice of the U.S. Supreme Court. He said, in an address to the American Bible Society that the Bible will **"inform them that our** gracious Creator has provided for us a Redeemer, in whom all the nations of the earth shall be blessed; that this Redeemer has made atonement 'for the sins of the whole world' . . ."[44] The Bible-driven Christianity of the Founders affected their politics, causing them to compose a Declaration of Independence, a Constitution and a Bill of Rights. Without Christianity none of these would be ours today. Liberty is rooted only in Christianity!

The church meeting in Colonial days was more liturgical and less inclined toward freedom of expression and emotional excesses. It was doctrinally orthodox; our Founders were more concerned with religious stability than with expressions of personal freedom. They were more interested in implanting responsibility in church members than having fun.

They were devoted to Christian Scriptures: When the Revolution cut off the supply of Bibles from England, Patrick Allison, Chaplain of Congress, placed before that body in 1777 a petition praying for immediate relief. A special Committee weighed the matter and, when it was brought before Congress, that body passed it on to a committee which reported that the use of the Bible was so universal and its importance so great that they recommended Congress authorize the importing of 20,000 Bibles from Holland, Scotland, or elsewhere, into the different parts of the States of the Union.[45] The same need arose three years later and, with approval from Congress, was filled by Robert Aitken, publisher of ***The Pennsylvania Magazine***. This began the publication of the ***Bible of the Revolution***. I ask: Is there a more worthy cause in which Congress might get involved?

Noah Webster, who himself found assurance of salvation at age fifty, said in his Moral Catechism that **"God's word . . . has furnished all necessary rules to direct our conduct."**[46]

One of the major concerns in Colonial America was their relationship with Native Americans. While the Indians were mistreated by fur traders and unscrupulous businessmen, the desire of Christian men was to bring them to faith in Jesus Christ. William Penn [1644-1718], the founder of Pennsylvania, had a good relationship with the Lenape [later called Delaware] tribe, signing a Treaty in 1682 that was never broken. Penn had come to faith in Christ as a teenager after living a sinful life. His father had been an Admiral in the King's Navy, and when he died the king owed him a large sum. To settle the account, King Charles II gave young William a tract of land in the New World. Penn called it Pennsylvania. He was known for his honest devotion to Jesus Christ, which was the reason he was trusted by the Lenape tribe.

As the Colonies expanded so did the need for a kind relation with the natives. The non-Christian attitude among settlers was to take advantage of the tribes; suppress them if necessary. Christians, on the other hand, worked for the conversion of the Indians. George Washington commended the Society of United Brethren for their **"endeavors to civilize and Christianize the Savages of the wilderness."** And to Rev. John Ettwein, Washington wrote regarding "converting the Indians to Christianity and consequently to civilization. . ."[47]

Noah Webster, in defining **savage**, quotes E.D. Griffin: **"What nation since the commencement of the Christian era, ever rose from savage to civilized without Christianity?"**[48] It was clearly understood by the Founders that there was a connection between **savage** and **non-Christian**, and between **civilized** and **Christianity**. They knew that winning the pagans to Jesus Christ would civilize them, which would be better than conquering them with the sword. The Founders came to understand that the key to man's needs was the truth as found in Jesus Christ. By *Christian* Webster meant, **"3. A real disciple of Christ; one who believes in the truth of the Christian religion, and studies to follow the example, and obey the precepts, of Christ; a believer in Christ who is characterized by real piety."**[49] It was the Christians who were the most concerned with the establishing of Liberty and Rights in society. And so, it was the Christians who were the driving force behind the establishing of that form of government that would best guarantee Rights. In fact, it was the Christian – like John Wesley, Charles Finney, and thousands more – who were most concerned with the Black man's Rights and fought to eliminate the scourge of slavery from America.

Because true Christians dominated the early political meetings and discussions, most of the elected delegates from the various Colonies were Christians: they had the greater sense of a need to be free to exercise Rights, especially the Right to worship.

Christianity was not simply near the heart of America: Christianity was the heart! This nation cannot be explained if Jesus Christ is avoided, belittled or exiled. Jesus Christ is very cordial and yielding: He will neither interfere nor stay where He is not wanted. When man labors on his own – and all his labors come to naught – he will then, hopefully, call out to Jesus Christ for aid.

The Christians of Early America started Harvard, Yale and the other institutions of higher learning. The Christians also started the American Bible Society, the Sunday School movement, related amiably with the American Indian, eventually headed up the fight against slavery, and promoted many other beneficial movements. The Christian needs to reexamine his relationship with government. But that can only be done in the midst of a personal Awakening when engulfed by the intense presence of God. Only there can we see clearly, for it is in His light that we see light. [Psalm 36:9; 43:3]

Jesus Christ was the Central person in Early America. Colonists did not "choose" him over other gods: He reigned – and still reigns – because of His authority in the world as the Son of God. Colonists did not confine Him to Sunday morning or lock Him behind Church doors. Jesus Christ must be welcomed in the public square, in the Court house, in the class room. He is King eternal, immortal, invisible, the only wise God [1 Tim.1:17]. Christianity is the Heart of Colonial America; Jesus Christ personally, providentially and powerfully sees to it that we are granted the Rights and Freedoms assigned to us by God and recorded in the Declaration of Independence.

One question remains: Have we lost heart?

6 – CAPITALISM IN COLONIAL AMERICA

Capitalism is an economic system wherein the means of production are privately owned, operated for profit, and where production, distribution, and the pricing of goods and services are determined by the desires and needs of society. Capitalism relies on the right of individuals and/or corporations to employ workers, trade, use money, labor, land and buildings to secure a profit. Capitalism means that the production and distribution of goods is governed by the free supply-and-demand market system, not by state regulation.

Capitalism and Christianity function best when in harmony with each other! Christianity fights for Rights, justice and impartiality. Capitalism, with its emphasis on free enterprise, functions properly where Christian honesty and a "do-unto-others-as-you-would-have-them-do-unto-you" principle lives unforced and spontaneously. The very essence of Capitalism is Free Enterprise. And that system operates and behaves only in a Capitalistic country. Capitalism has functioned so well in America for two centuries that, like Freedom itself, we hardly give it a second thought.

Freedom is intrinsic to Capitalism – and this creates a danger: It is possible to take advantage of the unsuspecting. Unscrupulous businessmen are not always rewarded in this life with due punishment. So the ambitious liberal, disturbed by what he sees, attempts to change the system into government-controlled socialism; and socialism eventually leads to communism. To the measure that Government controls commerce – to that measure Socialism invades the culture. It is Biblically essential to retain a free-market system, despite the built-in potential for greed and corruption. God Himself leaves man free to be selfish, to sin, even to forsake Him. Government dares not move away from its Founder: If God leaves men free, Government must do the same. There is a simple qualifier, however: Government protects all citizens equally: If a crime is committed against another member of society, Government is authorized by God, as Paul writes, *to execute wrath upon him who does evil, for Government does not bear the sword in vain.* [Rom.13:4] This is the legitimate role for government as authorized by God.

It is always hoped by liberals that governmental controls will eliminate corruption, greed and crime in the business world; that government is best suited to bring about equality in society. A look at the corruption and failures of the Communistic system should serve as an antidote for that sick idea.

Governments seek power to control and thereby steal authority from the people who either allow it to happen or rebel. Consider the economic relationship between England and the Colonists. John Hancock, an eventual signer of the Declaration of Independence, had his ship Liberty seized by the British in 1768, because he was smuggling tea without paying import taxes. John Adams defended him and the charges were eventually dropped, but Hancock, having several hundred more indictments against him, organized a boycott of tea from the East. Sales of British tea in the Colonies fell from 160 tons to ¼ ton, and Hancock continued importing tea from the Netherlands. As the British East India Company's tea piled up in warehouses, the British Government passed the Tea Act: This Act allowed the East India Company to sell tea to the colonies without paying customs or duties to Britain. This tax break allowed the East India Company to sell tea at half price and undercut the prices offered by Colonial merchants and smugglers. Britain's decision on customs and duties took the economy out of the "Free Enterprise" category – which always happens with government control. This is what led to the famed Boston Tea Party – discussed in a later chapter.

Throughout the history of America the temptation of Government is to expand. Whenever there are violations of laborers, a business, an individual or an organization, Government steps in with more laws to protect. However, laws that protect you or me invariably serve to deprive a segment of society of legitimate Freedoms. Any public official in early America who attempted to expand Government was quickly voted out of office. Today the politician who wants to be reelected grants special favors to his constituents at the expense of the free market economy. For example, the prime cause for the 2008 financial crisis on Wall Street can be laid at the door of Congress for encouraging Fannie Mae and Freddie Mac to back loans to low-income families that had not the wherewithal to repay. This liberal generosity on Barney Frank's part has kept him in Congress since

1981, but leaves the banking industry shaken. Forced equality plays havoc with America's Free Market economy, and is not guaranteed in the Constitution. Article 4 of the Bill of Rights states that the people have a right to be secure in their houses, but does not authorize government to provide the housing. . . There is greed on the heart of America's voters, and politicians know how to exploit that greed, promising to reward us with our neighbor's funds.

When Davy Crockett [1786-1836] was a member of the Tennessee legislature, a fire broke out down the street, destroying a military widow's home. The legislature voted to give her a measure of help. Sometime later when Crockett was running for re-election, he visited various families, hoping to secure their votes. When he came to farmer Bunce's home, the farmer said, **"No, I'll not vote for you!"** Crockett was surprised, but the farmer explained: **"Remember when you voted to give that widow some financial help? Well, you gave her my money! You may give your own money to her, but it was not right for you to give her mine."** Crockett agreed with Bunce, thanked him for the lesson in economics, and set out to convince the local farmers he would not do that again. Davy Crockett was elected to a second term in 1827, nine years before losing his life at the Alamo.

Sixty years later, in 1887, Democratic President Grover Cleveland vetoed a Texas Seed Bill. Here were the circumstances: After a drought had ruined crops in several Texas counties, Congress appropriated $10,000 to purchase seed grain for the distressed farmers. Cleveland vetoed the bill: He believed in the Capitalist system – and in limited government. Cleveland said: **"I can find no warrant for such an appropriation in the Constitution; and I do not believe that the power and duty of the General Government ought to be extended to the relief of individual suffering which is in no manner properly related to the public service or benefit. A prevalent tendency to disregard the limited mission of this power and duty should, I think, be steadily resisted . . ."[50]** Today it is no longer resisted, but welcomed!

Lest we think the veto came from a hard and unbelieving heart, we remind ourselves that it was this same President Cleveland who had a good handle on the relationship between Christianity, Capitalism and Government. Cleveland said: **"The citizen is a better business man if he is a Christian gentleman, and surely, business is not the less prosperous and successful if conducted on Christian principles. . . All must admit that the reception of the teachings of Christ results in the purest patriotism, in the most scrupulous fidelity to public trust, and in the best type of citizenship. Those who manage the affairs of government are by this means reminded that the law of God demands, that they should be courageously true to the interests of the people, and that the Ruler of the Universe will require of them a strict account of their stewardship. The teachings of both human and Divine law thus merging into one word, duty, form the only union of Church and state that a civil and religious government can recognize."[51]**

There is a relationship between the Ten Commandments and Capitalism: The 8th Commandment says: ***Thou shalt not steal!*** [Exodus 20:15] If this Commandment is violated, cutthroat commerce prevails. This Commandment requires absolute obedience. The Christian businessman functions in a world of absolute standards without having to persistently assess his deeds. He need not ask himself, **Did I steal or did I not steal from my customer on that deal?** If he is a true Christian, his godly nature carries him beyond self-analysis and into spontaneous honesty in his business life. And if selfish motives rise to the surface in his life, the Holy Spirit compels immediate correction. If the Spirit does not, he must proceed to a thorough examination to determine if he is really in the faith.

Communism is – by its very nature – opposed to both Christianity and Capitalism. The Communist system was attempted in the Plymouth Colony for the first two years. The Colonists on Plymouth Plantation brought all their produce into one common storehouse, and it was then dispersed as needs arose. This sounded "Christian" in its inception, but the system soon triggered greed and lethargy. With greed comes the accusation that others are getting more than they deserve, as well as the feeling on the part of some that they were more deserving for working harder, or longer, or better. Once the Plymouth Plantation went to Capitalism in 1623 and each family had their own plot of ground for planting, cultivating and harvesting for their own use, ambition returned and productivity increased to a significant and satisfactory level.

Communism attempts to prohibit selfishness, but here too it utterly fails. Prior to the collapse of the Soviet Union about five percent of the land was worked by homeowners in their own back yards, or wherever they could find a vacant field. Those five percent produced about 95% of the goods on the Russian market. All this while potatoes were rotting in government storage: Whether a man worked or not; whether the storage manager got the potatoes to market or not, he was paid his "equal" share. While rich Hollywood liberals bash the Free Enterprise system in America, they will surely not appreciate the next step – Communism – where they will receive the same pay as the factory worker. After Communism fell in the Soviet Union, waitresses in restaurants often sat in the back room while customers waited to be served: They were not acquainted with Free Enterprise where service generates success.

The best form of Government is a democratic republic! The reason is simple: A democratic republic leaves men free to pursue their own interests on their own property. Men will make mistakes in the process – but that is essential in living a responsible lives. God Himself leaves men free to believe in His Son, or to selfishly reject Him: God does not force conversions with the sword, as do Moslem, but He anoints His servants with His Spirit to present the Gospel of forgiveness and grace through Jesus Christ.

Like the human body which requires certain ingredients to sustain life, there are also essentials in maintaining life in the body politic. A primary ingredient in a republic is *public virtue*. According to Forrest McDonald, *public virtue* meant **"firmness, courage, endurance, industry, frugal living, strength, and above all, unremitting devotion to . . . the community of virtuous men. . ."** McDonald adds: **If public virtue declined, the republic declined, and if it declined too far, the republic died."[52]**

When men are free to pursue and develop their interests in a righteous way, the Providential hand of God works with them, rewarding or punishing or nudging, not toward success but toward the development of a godly character. Consider the case of George Washington Carver [1864-1943], a black man who asked God one simple question: **"Please, Mr. Creator, will you tell me why the peanut was made?"** Out of Carver's question came the answer: 325 uses for the peanut, including beverages, cosmetics, dies, paints, stains, animal foods, people foods, medicines and other general uses such as cleaners, fuels, etc. Carver explained his achievement as follows: **"The secret of my success? It is simple. It is found in the Bible, 'In all thy ways acknowledge Him and He shall direct thy paths'."[53]**

No other economic system could force or convince Carver to be energized in developing so many products from the simple peanut. Without freedom it would not have happened! Freedom in this case is the opposite of law, for no law could be employed to energize the psychological desire or mental capacity to do what Carver did. Such is the result when the Spirit of God directs the believer – and when the Capitalistic system is in place and promoted by Congress and Court alike.

The Colonial Founders, who structured our Declaration of Independence and Constitution, had no idea of the extent they were contributing to the individual's success and freedom, and therefore the success of the whole nation. The Founders were simply doing what they determined was an act of obedience to principles disclosed in the writings of Montesquieu[54] and Locke[55] and many others, including Blackstone and the Book of Deuteronomy. While many are looking for change, this is the change we need – a return to the foundations upon which this country was founded and which made it great! If we leave the Capitalistic system for more governmental control, we will have jeopardized Freedom, Christianity and even curbed the Hand of Providence. God Himself functions in Freedom, and has ordained that man do the same!

The Christian must fight tenaciously for Capitalism because it is intricately tied into our Rights and Freedoms. If we lose Capitalism in favor of Socialism – and then Communism, its perpetual and permanent friend, we will lose religious freedom and speech freedom. It is understandable why Dietrich Bonhoeffer would face down the Gestapo in 1942 and **"openly admitted that, as a Christian, he was a relentless enemy of National Socialism . . ."[56]** If we expect Providence to work on our behalf, our battle against the Socialistic trends today must be as firm and relentless as Bonhoeffer's stand on behalf of the German nation.

We hear again the Lord God asking: *Can these bones live again?* We pray so!

7 – INDEPENDENCE IN COLONIAL AMERICA

Independence was in the mind of God, for it put both the individual and the nation in a place where obedience to His Law could be carried out. If a man was a slave of another he could not fulfill his duty to God – if the slave-master hindered him in doing so. A nation that was bound by and dependent on another nation could not—as in the case of America—fulfill its duty to God.

If it meant War in order for Independence to be secured – so be it! Though Britain possessed colonies around the world – Canada, India, Australia, New Zealand and about ninety more – Britain would not give up her potentially most valuable colonies in America. This was much like a teen-age son who decides to be free from controls by moving out of his parents' home. This is especially troubling to the parents when the teen-ager contributes a good share to the family budget. In addition, every time the son turns around his parents extract more funds from his McDonald's pay check. They feel the son needs to appreciate what they have done for him over the years, how they struggled to bring him into existence. Continually loading him with financial burdens simply drives the son and the parents further apart. They feel he should love them; they demand that he love them – out of sheer duty. In addition, they demand that he goes to their church.

The British Parliament tried to control break-away religions by passing what they called a

"Conventicle Act." [Conventicle means meeting or assembly.] There were three basic Conventicle Acts: The first [1593] required all separatists to be Church of England Anglicans: Those who refused were executed or exiled. The second Conventicle Act [1664] prohibited religious meetings of more than five people—unless the meeting was approved by the Church of England. The third Act [1670] imposed fines for anyone attending a religious meeting, and a heavier fine on any person who allowed his home to be used for such a meeting. Fines were double for second offenses.[70]

In addition to religious oppression there was excessive taxation. Soon there were taxes on items like Molasses [1733], Sugar [1764] and Stamps [1765]. When tea marketed by the East India Company was rotting in India and China warehouses, Britain agreed not to tax their tea. It was to be sold in America for half the price that Colonial merchants charged for their tea. This of course would ruin the Colonial economy. Protest meetings were held, many of them organized by Samuel Adams, the cousin of our Second President, John Adams.

Ships arrived in Boston Harbor carrying tea. Colonists refused to let the tea be unloaded. The owner of the first ship, the ***Dartmouth***, agreed to leave the harbor with his tea, but Governor Hutchinson, appointed by Britain to oversee Boston, refused to let it leave Boston Harbor. Soon the protest meeting had grown to an estimated 8,000 people. Upon a signal from Sam Adams on Dec.19, 1773, the Sons of Liberty proceeded to the British ships and dumped

342 chests of tea into Boston Harbor waters. Each chest weighed about 260 pounds. The total value was close to two million dollars, but obviously much more on today's market. This infuriated the British beyond measure; they blockaded Boston Harbor: No goods could be shipped in or out. Prior to this event, needed goods were exported and imported through Boston Harbor, including thousands of pounds of tea, smuggled into the Colonies, duty free. But all shipping stopped! Should America yield?

To understand the Colonial attitude, consider a sermon by Rev. Ebenezer Baldwin, a Yale graduate and pastor of a Danbury church on August 31, 1774. As the Revolution began, many Episcopal pastors went back to England. However, Pastor Baldwin's sermon expressed a growing sentiment among many pastors who aligned themselves with Freedom's cause. Baldwin addressed the issue of taxes, land rights, trials by jury, religious tyranny and foreign soldiers housed in American homes. He said in a sermon, abbreviated here, that **"men accustomed to freedom cannot realize all the horrors of slavery. We must either submit to such a dreadful state of slavery or must by force and arms stand up in defense of our liberties."** He concluded by saying: **"May Americans be united in a just sense of the worth of their civil rights and in every laudable and righteous method for obtaining redress; and God grant their struggles in so glorious a cause may be crowned with happy success."**[57]

While only 56 delegates signed the Declaration of Independence – a few reluctantly – the majority of delegates, and a majority of the people, knew there was no other route to take. The Providence of God was on their side. The Churches were for independence, which meant freedom of worship. For example, when Rev. Peter Muhlenberg went from Pennsylvania to Virginia to preach, he had to first get his ordination from the Church of England—even though he was a Lutheran preacher. The merchants and farmers and common folks were for independence because of the oppressive controls of the British soldiers, British-appointed judges and growing taxation. However, there are still some today who question whether it was right to break from Britain. Submission under all circumstances is the argument they use. For these we suggest the reading of Pastor Baldwin's sermon. When speaking of slavery he warned, **there is no telling what men will soon become when entrusted with arbitrary power: such power will more surely intoxicate men than the strongest spirits: the best of men cannot be safely trusted with it. Many men amiable in private life have become monsters of cruelty when entrusted with arbitrary power: such were many of the Roman emperors.**[58]

A major issue that faced the Colonies pertained to land ownership. To review history – in the year 1066, William the Norman [from Normandy on the coast of France], invaded and conquered England. In doing so all England became his personal possession; land, buildings, rivers, commerce, people. This began the feudal system in which the King owned all. He charged rents from his under-lords who in turn used serfs to work his land and fight his wars. All belonged to the King by **"right of conquest."**

Now, 700 years later, the King of England was still convinced everything belonged to him, including America. This policy was called **"the divine right of kings."** Britain determined to control Colonial economy; tax to whatever degree he chose; remove rights and privileges when he felt it necessary; restrict and regulate worship; dismiss the British Parliament or Colonial officials if they opposed him; place soldiers in private Colonial homes; confiscate guns when he saw his authority was threatened; and removed Colonial charters at a whim. All this because the King thought he **owned** the Colonies. So, when King Charles II, in 1683, demanded the return of the Massachusetts charter, the pastor, Increase Mather, objected. [Note: A Colonial Charter, issued by some competent British authority, is a document that gave a Colony the legal right to exist.] Pastor Mather, who oversaw the Colony of Puritans, responded by declaring: **"To submit and resign their charter would be inconsistent with the main end of their fathers' coming to New England. . . [although resistance would provoke] great sufferings, [it is] better to suffer than sin."**[59] They had left Old England to be free to worship and please God in New England according to conscience. To do otherwise was sin! If the King retained possession of the land, they well understood that he also owned them. Independence was looking very logical to them at this point!

The War for Independence was primarily a war over property ownership! John Locke

[1632-1704], mentioned earlier, wrote, **"The great and chief end, therefore, of man's uniting into commonwealths, and putting themselves under government, is the preservation of their property. . ."** He concluded, **"Every person has property in his own person."**[60] That is, every man owns himself! This was not a policy created by the Continental Congress or authorized by the King or Parliament; it was granted by God and established in the Colonies at the time of the Great Awakening. It was called the Law of Nature.

The king's false assumption was that he owned everything and everyone. Thomas Jefferson was also aware of the King's false notion, and said, **"America was not conquered by William the Norman, nor its lands surrendered to him or any of his successors. Possessions there [in America] are undoubtedly of the allodial nature."** [61]

The allodial system of land ownership is the opposite of the feudal system. In feudalism the King was the final owner; in the allodial system the citizen held final ownership. Consider a Pennsylvania case wherein Judge Woodward spelled out his reasoning on America's Revolution. In that case the judge declared: **"We are then to regard the Revolution . . . as emancipating every acre of the soil of Pennsylvania from the grand characteristic of the feudal system."** Allodial, on the other hand, was a word meaning **"owned free of any superior claim, without rent or payment."**[62]

Interestingly enough, but not surprising, the word **allodial** no longer appears in college dictionaries.

The reason is obvious: There is no more **allodial** land ownership in America. Government is the superior! The proof of this is seen when a land owner dies in absence of a will, and no heir is found. In that case land reverts back to the state. It is also seen in the fact that the land owner pays taxes on the home he owns. Why? Government is the final owner!

The King of England was not about to yield control of the American Colonies: Oppression of the Colonies became so great that even some in Parliament opposed British tyranny. Bishop Jonathan Shipley told his colleagues in the House of Lords in 1774 that **"we force every North American to be our enemy . . . It is a strange idea we have taken up, to cure their resentments by increasing provocation. . . That just God, whom we have all so deeply offended, can hardly inflict a severer national punishment than by committing us to the natural consequences of our own conduct."**[63] This was also the conviction of Edmund Burke who, in addressing the House of Commons in 1777 said, **"The question with me is not whether you have a right to render your people miserable, but whether it is not your interest to make them happy. Perhaps we might wish the colonists to be persuaded that their liberty is more secure when held in trust for them by us . . . than with any part of it in their own hands.** Then Burke bitingly adds: **"An Englishmen is the unfittest person on earth to argue another Englishman into slavery."**[64] But that is what Britain determined to do!

Parliament would not listen to the arguments of Shipley and Burke. Tyranny continued! Pastor Mayhew of Boston had preached in 1750 that, **"It is blasphemy to call tyrants and oppressors God's ministers. . . When [magistrates] rob and ruin the public, instead of being guardians of its peace and welfare, they immediately cease to be the ordinance and ministers of God, and no more deserve that glorious character than common pirates and highwaymen."**[65]

Fifteen years later Pastor Mayhew declared, **". . . as soon as the prince sets himself above the law, he does, to all intents and purposes, un-king himself by acting out of and beyond that sphere which the constitution allows. . ."**[66] This was also the teaching in **<u>Rex Lex</u>** [or, **<u>The Law and the Prince</u>**], written by Samuel Rutherford [1600-1661] of Scotland to show that the King is subject to law as much as are the people. Anyone possessing a copy of Rutherford's book at that time in the British Empire was treated as an enemy of the government.[67]

Disrespect for the King of England was growing. His arbitrary rulings were troublesome in the Colonies. As early as 1768, William Livingstone, well-known New York lawyer and one of the eventual delegates to the Constitutional Convention, said: **"Courage, Americans . . . The finger of God points out a mighty empire to your sons. The land we possess is the gift of heaven. The day dawns in which the foundation of this mighty empire is to be laid . . . before seven years roll over our heads, the first stone must be laid."**[68] This was quoted in the *New*

York Gazette in April, 1768. Seven years later, to the very month, April of 1775, **"the shot heard round the world"** was fired on Lexington Green. War for freedom had begun!

It was indeed heard round the world, for nations like Germany and France sent help to the Colonies in their struggle for Independence. It was a shot that is still heard – and still calls the world's masses to a freedom found nowhere else. Sadly, however, we have forgotten the price that was paid on our behalf— and forgotten how to retain that Independence.

There are times when we stubbornly clung to the Declaration of Independence as though it will save us, forgetting that this Document, having flowed from the Great Awakening, was alive in the hearts of men like Washington, Adams and Webster and – for that matter – the general populous. The Documents, without being instilled in the lives of men, were merely ink on paper. It was the men – and the women – who made the Declaration work. Independence was a living principle in flesh and blood lives.

Are there men and women today who will make it work again? *Can these bones live again?*

SECTION II –

PRESCRIPTION FOR HEALTH

———

While the term, *The West*, has several meanings, for our purposes *The West* originated with Jesus Christ and the westward move of the Gospel, beginning more specifically with Paul's ministry in Antioch, then Macedonia, and eventually Europe, England and America. While *The West* refers to those lands west of Israel, the birthplace of Jesus Christ, *The East* refers to those countries that lie east of Israel. Jesus Christ, being the Head of the Church, authorized this westward move, and all spiritual life and health begins with and resides in Him.

In the first 300 years of the westward move, the Church was healthy. Deep persecution kept the Church relatively pure: Why would anyone join if it meant losing their life? Roman Emperor Constantine stopped persecution around 310; in 325 Christianity was accepted, though other religions were permitted;

in 380 Emperor Theodosius made Christianity the official religion of the Roman Empire. Because the masses of people were brought into the Church, the Church died spiritually. Instead of winning the lost, the Church persecuted those who refused to join. In the early 1500s Martin Luther of Germany created a spiritual stir. From there the Gospel began again its move toward *The West* – first England and then America.

Dietrich Bonhoeffer states that the American Revolution, 1775-1783, was based **"upon the kingdom of God and the limitation of all earthly powers by the sovereignty of God. The federal constitution was written by men who were conscious of original sin and of the wickedness of the human heart."** Near this same time the French Revolution [1789-1799] took place. It was based on a document called **Declaration of the Rights of Man** which states, **"The origin of all sovereignty lies in the nation."** God was excluded! Lawlessness reigned!

As these two declarations – the French **Declaration of the Rights of Man** and the American **Declaration of Independence** – drew followers during the past 200+ years, secular man has been increasingly drawn to the French idea. Bonhoeffer laments, **"What the west is doing is to refuse to accept its historical inheritance for what it is. The west is becoming hostile towards Christ. This is the peculiar situation of our time, and it is genuine decay. Amidst the disruption of the whole established order of things there stand the**

Christian Churches as guardians of the heritage of the Middle Ages and of the Reformation and especially as witnesses of the miracle of God in Jesus Christ yesterday, and today, and forever [Hebrews 13:8]. The world has turned its back on Christ, and it is to this world that the Church must now prove that Christ is the living Lord. The more central the message of the Church, the greater now will be her effectiveness.[69]

Across the American landscape are scattered faithful pastors who are unconcerned with fame and unmoved by the motivational orator who beckons him with five keys to bigness. This faithful shepherd has found his sole contentment in pleasing Jesus – watching the sheep, over which he has been made overseer, grow in grace and the true knowledge of Jesus Christ.

8 – THE GREAT AWAKENING

Had there been no Great Awakening there would not have been a United States of America. Without the groundwork laid in the American culture by the Awakening, there would have been no **Declaration of Independence**. There may have been a **Declaration of the Rights of Man** like the one drawn up by the French for their revolution, a man-exalting declaration that cost the lives of more than 40,000 Frenchmen; a document that soon faded into nothingness. Without the Declaration of Independence there would have been no U.S. Constitution – no Bill of Rights – and no Liberty! God blessed America with men who knew how to put God's preferences down on paper!

Colonial Christianity can only be understood in the light of the Great Awakening that affected the Colonies from Georgia to New England. For that matter, it is not an overstatement to say that nothing in the development of America can be accurately understood apart from that Awakening. This spiritual Awakening occurred from 1739-1742, and became the standard by which all other Revivals are measured.

Many lives were changed under the preaching of Jonathan Edwards [1703-1758], George Whitefield [1714-1770], and a multitude of other compelling preachers whose message of redemption in Jesus Christ changed lives. The Great Awakening went far beyond the salvation of individual souls. It went beyond the growth of the churches. It went even beyond the personal assurance and peace enjoyed by those who came to faith in Jesus Christ. **The impact**

of the Great Awakening can only be appreciated when we consider the world before 1740 and the world after 1740! Prior to that year the intellectual world in Europe and America was scholastic, authoritarian and stagnant. The Church of England attempted to dominate religious observances: The Church of England's Prayer Book was used because only the Church of England was considered legitimate. This was especially true in Virginia. Within about ten years following the Awakening, a total break from the mediaeval world of Europe had taken place in America. Bondage was gone! People were inwardly free: They worshipped Jesus Christ anew, and they saw their world in a new way. It was a world that Christ came to redeem – and Colonists began loving one another. The Spirit of God had breathed new life into dry bones: Men were alive to God!

America would not and could not be brought back under bondage. The souls of men were free, and therefore free to think God's thoughts about Rights and Liberty and loyalties. No longer would Government be their god: That place in individual lives as well as in American culture was now reserved for Jesus Christ alone.

As stated above, the Great Awakening produced personal Freedom, the groundwork for the **Declaration of Independence**. Soon there would be a U.S. Constitution, then a Bill of Rights, then a nation that flowed with peace and safety. God blessed America with men who knew how to know God's will in this matter. Lest we exalt man beyond what they deserve, I believe that what they put together was even beyond the Framers' wisdom and intentions. Had there been no Hand of Providence and no spiritual Awakening, it simply would never have happened!

Our Independence and Constitution came about, not simply because free governments need religion, and religion needs free government. It came about because the intellectual world, the schools, and even the common man were set free from stagnation. Jesus Christ sets people free, not to use their liberty *"as an opportunity for the flesh,"* but as an occasion to *"serve one another,"* [Galatians 5:13] and this was happening in America. The bondage prior to 1740 was primarily a religious bondage that was an authoritarian domination of people; not just over their external lives, but it was a repressive squelching of personal initiative and energy. Whatever energy the church did not squeeze from the lives of people, the state did. Bonhoeffer observes: **"It cannot be overlooked that technology has arisen only in the west, that is to say, in the world which has been shaped by Christianity . . . Emancipated reason acquired mastery over creation and so led to the triumph of technical science. The age of technology is a genuine heritage of our western history."**[70]

There was a time when the Bible was virtually banned – even in progressive England. People were starving for a word from God – but they did not even know they were starving. They had not been taught that personal salvation was available to the one who came directly to Jesus Christ for the forgiveness of sin. The Roman Church, and then the British Church, each saw themselves as the door to heaven. The Reformation broke that door open, but it was the Great Awakening that once and for all blew it off its hinges, never to be re-installed.

A dominant feature of the Great Awakening was the centrality of the Bible and the preached Word. The servant whom God used was secondary. When people came to hear Edwards or Whitefield they were not smitten by the speaker's eloquence; they were individually and personally confronted by the Spirit of God regarding sin and righteousness. Among today's purveyors of religious information and excitement, the speaker and his program is central; all else is secondary. Jesus, in many church settings, stands on the sidelines as a quiet observer. The preacher's emotions and methods dominate the religious stage; the Word is misshapen and perverted so that the personal ends of the speaker might be achieved: Prominence, applause and a goodly bank account! Not so in the Great Awakening – for God does not use the arrogant or the one who robs Him of His glory.

Benjamin Franklin, a personal friend of George Whitefield, in his autobiography, wrote on the effects of the Great Awakening: *"It was wonderful to see the change soon made in the manners of our inhabitants. From being thoughtless or indifferent about religion, it seemed as if all the world were growing religious, so that one could not walk thro' the town in an evening without hearing psalms sung in different families of every street."*[71]

Another effect of the Great Awakening is still prevalent today: Charities, volunteerism and aid that pours from America into all parts of the world is beyond anything any other nation has produced. Doctors and nurses, engineers and missionaries, relief agencies and aid workers of every sort cover the globe in an effort to bring comfort and help to a needy world – all this had its beginnings in the Great Spiritual Awakening that brought life to a nation and introduced spontaneity into America's social responsibilities.

While the Great Awakening slammed the door shut on the old Mediaeval World, it opened a whole New World of Liberty and sealed to us our Rights, the Right to walk with God according to Conscience, the Right to be Self-Governing, and the Right to form a new Government designed to protect those Rights. This New World was called America! It was an experiment that had never been tried! Would it work?

The views of John Calvin [1509-1564] were still of the Middle Ages. He generally believed that each person in society had an assigned role: Leaders were to lead and followers were to follow, but followers should not interfere with leaders, even if leaders erred. It was God's role to correct them when they were out of order. Although the primary preachers during the Awakening, including Edwards and Whitefield, were Calvinists, the Great Awakening broke American society free from the harsher views of John Calvin, bringing a new freedom to the common man, a freedom that strict Calvinism did not offer. Under the effective preaching of Edwards and Whitefield, hyper-Calvinism was arrested and a new Evangelicalism was instituted on the American frontier. The results of Edwards' and Whitefield's preaching went, I believe, even beyond their intentions – and that was indeed a good thing.

Changes were also taking place in the schools of higher learning. The Awakening shook Harvard [v.1636] as well as Yale [b.1701]. These schools had become elitist, snobby and stale. Actually, Yale was started because Harvard was becoming spiritually dead by 1701. But Yale, Harvard's younger sister, soon followed in her older sister's ways. For instance, though Yale had glorious beginnings, by the 1720's several Yale teachers & students rejected the vibrancy of Puritanism and went back to the austere and stately Episcopal [Anglican] church.

Whenever there is a religious revival or even one person's conversion, the question arises: What brought that about? This is particularly true when looking at the Great Awakening that swept many into the Kingdom of God and changed the general attitude of society.

The process toward spiritual barrenness happened over many years: Martin Luther had brought about a great Reformation in Germany which affected all of Europe including England. But England, which had split from Rome, still retained a liturgical and formal way of approaching God. England had never been delivered from Rome's formalism. The churches in America, even those not Anglican, brought with them the same formalistic attitude toward life, politics, church and God. To borrow from Calvin – everyone kept their place; that was all that was expected of them.

Protestants were increasingly concerned with America's sterility. European rationalism prevailed, leading to naturalism. (Rationalism is any view that appeals to reason as a source of knowledge; Naturalism is the idea that the unaided natural mind can figure out what is real.) The Rationalist and the Naturalist saw material as the basis of reality, with no room for the spirit of man: the Christian sees Spirit as the basis of all reality. Naturalism leads inescapably and predictably to spiritual sterility and death: It does not and cannot meet the needs of man. To deny the existence of the spirit does not meet the need: It is like denying the existence of the chair on which you are sitting. The hunger among preachers and laymen alike opened the hearts of men for an Awakening.

Edwards believed the millennium would come gradually, that the people of God were capable of *"falling in"* with God's plan. This introduced a *"historical optimism"* that was a lasting legacy of the Great Awakening. Instead of worshipping a God who was removed and unapproachable, Christians found God to be very near [Acts 17:27]. Obviously believers found the same teaching in the Bible [recall that the Bible was the first book printed on Gutenberg's press around 1450, and soon thousands were printed across Europe and America.] This new-found liberty had a profound influence on the church in America as it broke away from typical Calvinism, mainstream Anglicanism and stifling Romanism.

Rationalism and Naturalism did all it could to destroy faith in Jesus and peace with God. However, to the measure that the Bible is embraced in the hearts of men, society is changed, and Rationalism and Naturalism fade away. The Bible was the foundation for what transpired in the Awakening, as well as the foundation for what was to follow – eventually even the Declaration of Independence. During America's formative years – 1760-1805 – the Bible was the most quoted source of information by the Founders.[72]

Thomas Jefferson wrote that the reason Christianity is the best friend of government is because Christianity is the only religion that changes the heart. And George Washington said it is impossible to rightly govern the world without God and the Bible. George Washington was about ten years of age when the Great Awakening occurred. His mother and young George were obviously greatly affected by the Biblical preaching of that day.

To say that George Whitefield's ministry was dynamic is an understatement. To get a feel for the impact of Whitefield, consider the following account of a Nathan Cole who attended Whitefield's meeting at Middletown, CT., on Oct. 23, 1740. The report of Cole shows us what was going on in the Colonies as men and women were constrained by an irresistible force as the Providence of God was preparing America for freedom. To lay it all on Edwards and Whitefield is to fail to understand the working of the Spirit of God. Here is Cole's commentary:

Now it pleased God to send Mr. Whitefield into this land, and many thousands flocking to

hear him preach the Gospel, and great numbers were converted to Christ. I felt the Spirit of God drawing me by conviction: I longed to see and hear him and wished he would come this way. I had heard he was to come to New York and the Jerseys – next he was at Long Island, then at Boston, and next at Northampton. Then on a sudden about 8 or 9 of the clock there came a messenger and said Mr. Whitefield is to preach at Middletown this morning at ten of the clock. I was in my field at work. I dropped my tool and ran home to my wife, telling her to make ready quickly to hear Mr. Whitefield preach, then ran to my pasture for my horse with all my might, fearing I should be too late. I with my wife soon mounted and went forward as fast as I thought the horse could bear, and when my horse got much out of breath I would get down and put my wife on the saddle and bid her ride as fast as she could and not stop or slack until I bade her, and so I would run until I was much out of breath and then mount my horse again, and so I did several times to favor my horse. We improved to get along as if we were fleeing for our lives, all the while fearing we should be too late to hear the sermon, for we had twelve miles to ride in little more than an hour. When we came within about a mile of the road that comes from Harford to Middletown, I saw before me a cloud of fog arising. I first thought it came from the great [Connecticut] river, but as I came nearer the road I heard a noise of horses' feet coming down the road, and this cloud was a cloud of dust made by the horses' feet. It arose into the air over the tops of hills and trees; and when I came within about 300 feet of the road, I could see men and horses slipping along in the cloud like shadows, and as I drew nearer it seemed like a steady stream of horses and their riders, scarcely a horse more than his length behind another, all of a lather and foam with sweat, their breath rolling out of their nostrils every jump. Every horse seemed to go with all his might to carry his rider to hear news from heaven for the saving of souls. It made me tremble to see the sight, how the world was in a struggle. I found a vacancy between two horses to slip in mine and my wife said, 'Law, our clothes will be all spoiled, see how they look,' for they were so covered with dust that they looked all of a color, coats, hats, shirts and horse. We went down in the stream but heard no man speak a word all the way for 3 miles but everyone pressing forward in great haste; and when we got to Middletown old meeting house there was 3 or 4,000 people assembled. We dismounted and shook off our dust. I turned and looked towards the Great River and saw the ferry boats running swift backward and forward bringing over loads of people, and the oars rowed nimbler and quick. Everything, men, horses, and boats seemed to be struggling for life. The land and banks over the river looked black with people and horses; all along the 12 miles I saw no man at work in his field. When I saw Mr. Whitefield come upon the scaffold, he looked almost angelical; a young [27-years old], slim, youth, before some thousands of people with a bold undaunted countenance. And my hearing how God was with him everywhere as he came along, it solemnized my mind and put me into a trembling fear before he began to preach; for he looked as if he was clothed with authority from the Great God, and a sweet solemn solemnity sat upon his brow, and my hearing him preach gave me a heart wound. But God's blessing, my old foundation was broken up, and I saw that my righteousness would not save me.[73]

Nathan Cole had attended Whitefield's meeting in Middletown in October of 1740. He later reported, **"I was born Feb. 15th 1711 and born again Octo 1741."**[74] The work of redemption was complete in Cole one year after hearing Whitefield at Middletown. Whitefield was not concerned with counting conversions: if it took a year of seeking, that would be better for Cole than to give him false assurance.

A while after the Great Awakening, Jonathan Edwards gave a lengthy report in which he wrote how God was remarkably present amongst them by His Holy Spirit; adding that there was no Book so delightful as the Bible; especially the Book of Psalms, the Prophecy of Isaiah, and the New Testament. Edwards explains that there will be **very dark before the work of God begins**. When the Spirit of God moves on the land it will not only be **a time of great light and knowledge**, but also **a time of great holiness**. It will be a time when **religion is uppermost in the world**, and **times of great peace** and love; and it will be **a time of excellent order in the church of Christ.** All of these things were taking place in America during the Great Awakening. The nation had moved from deep spiritual darkness to brilliance, so that it prompted Edwards to conclude that **"this is most properly the time of the kingdom of heaven upon earth,"** and: **"Now is the principal fulfillment of all the prophecies of the Old Testament** [regarding] **the latter days."**[75]

This same feeling seemed to flow on into the hearts of the Founders thirty years later. As the Declaration of Independence was being signed in 1776, Samuel Adams said: **"We have this day restored the Sovereign to Whom all men ought to be obedient. He reigns in heaven and from the rising to the setting of the sun, let His kingdom come."**[76] Yet, they were not so naïve as to think America could not lapse again into spiritual darkness. John Quincy Adams, our Sixth President, was more spiritually perceptive than his father, John Adams, our Second President. J.Q. Adams said in 1814: **"Posterity – you will never know how much it has cost my generation to preserve your freedom. I hope you will make good use of it."** [77]

For any who might wonder if there were lingering effects of the Great Awakening on American culture, consider the analysis of Alexis de Tocqueville [1805-1859], a French statesman and historian. He had toured America in 1831 – almost a century after the Great Awakening, and 55 years after the signing of the Declaration of Independence. Here is a bit of his report entitled ***Democracy in America***, revealing the lasting effects the Great Awakening had on American culture. De Tocqueville asserts, in part:

Upon my arrival in the United States the religious aspect of the country was the first thing that struck my attention . . . In the United States the sovereign authority is religious . . .

There is no country in the world where the Christian religion retains a greater influence over the souls of men than in America, and there can be no greater proof of its utility and of its conformity to human nature than that its influence is powerfully felt over the most enlightened and free nation of the earth.

I sought for the key to the greatness and genius of America in her harbors ... in her fertile fields and boundless forests ... in her rich mines and vast world commerce ... in her public school system and institutions of learning. I sought for it in her democratic Congress and in her matchless Constitution. Not until I went into the churches of America and heard her pulpits flame with righteousness did I understand the secret of her genius and power.

America is great because America is good, and if America ever ceases to be good, America will cease to be great.

Christianity, therefore, reigns without obstacle, by universal consent."[78]

The Spirit breathed life into dry bones, and by the powerful Hand of Providence those bones became a mighty army, a mighty nation under God!

9 – THE BATTLE PLAN

Britain brought both religious and political pressure to bear against the Colonies, and it was having dire effects. When the British passed the Tea Act, intended to undercut the local economy, the Colonists, on December 16, 1773, dumped British tea into Boston Harbor. So Britain blockaded Boston Harbor. To determine a proper Colonial response, a Continental Congress was convened in Philadelphia with delegates from the Thirteen Colonies: That was on September 5, 1774 – and met [about twenty times] whenever business called for it until they turned their records over to the new Congress on July 25, 1789, on orders of President George Washington. It was this Continental Congress that approved the final draft of the Declaration of Independence on July 4, 1776.

Now—what would the British do? Go back to England? Four thousand of their soldiers were occupying homes in the Philadelphia area, many of them housed in Colonial homes. The British were in charge – they thought. Going home would mean voluntarily giving up tax income that rightly belonged to the Crown – they thought. Less than 200 years earlier they had totally destroyed the Spanish Armada: Now, if they packed their bags and went home, they would lose face before the whole world.

The British determined to stay and fight. The Colonies too would not back down. The battle would soon be joined. British troops headed for Lexington and Concord to capture Colonial weapons and ammunition in secret stashes on the night of April

18, 1775; merchants and farmers resisted the attack. This was the beginning of the War for Independence. The Colonies exercised great patience, hoping and appealing for reconciliation with Britain, but Parliament held firm. It would be more than one year before all avenues were exhausted—and the only way was a Declaration of Independence. The British fought for ownership of American land, produce, tax revenue and church loyalty. The Colonists would fight for Liberty, the Right to worship, and the Freedom to order their own affairs.

Thomas Paine, the author of Common Sense, came on the American scene with a different spirit than Americans had found in the Great Awakening. He did not have much influence on the future direction of the Colonies: He had come from France on Nov.30, 1774, almost three months after the First Continental Congress had met in Philadelphia. The structure was already in place for a righteous split with Great Britain. It was a split that was firmly fixed on Christianity, the signers of the Declaration being primarily Christians. Paine was not, even though he had been born to Quaker parents. Ours was a Revolution against lawlessness, and was for the purpose of establishing law; the French and Paine pushed lawlessness.

Francis Schaeffer states that the French **Declaration of the Rights of Man** sounded fine, but it had nothing to rest upon except the selfishness of man. Schaeffer asserts that in the French **Declaration** 'the Supreme Being' equaled 'the sovereignty of the nation'—that is, the general will of the people.

This was far different than the U.S. Declaration of Independence. Schaffer points out that the **American Declaration** was based on the Reformation, the **French Declaration** had no base.[79]

Within a short time France's **Declaration** was a dead document: it had no life from the outset. Soon 40,000 people died in the struggle: the devastation coming not from an outside enemy: The carnage was produced by the anti-god system. On the other hand, the **U.S. Declaration of Independence,** still valid, was not based on man's opinions but on timeless and undying principles. That **Declaration** is in keeping with both the nature of God and the nature of man.

That which inspired the Colonists more than Paine's Common Sense was **Vindiciae Contra Tyrranos,** *[A Defense of Liberty Against Tyrants.]* It was written by Mornay under the pen-name Junius Brutus in 1579. It was a book John Adams held to be one of the more influential books in America on the eve of the Revolution. **Vindiciae Contra Tyrranos** was foundational, holding, among other things that, **"First, Any ruler who commands anything contrary to the law of God thereby forfeits his realm. Second, Rebellion is refusal to obey God, for we ought to obey God rather than man. To obey the ruler when he commands what is against God's law is thus truly rebellion. Third, since God's law is the fundamental law and the only true source of law . . . neither king nor subject is exempt from it..."[80]**

British control of the Colonies became unbearable, especially when by force of arms she attempted to control Colonial economy. The Colonists appealed to the King, but to no avail. When British troops fired upon the farmers who had gathered on Lexington Green in defense of their property, the battle began. Patrick Henry, in his famous speech before a Convention of delegates at St. John's Church, Richmond, Virginia, on March 23, 1775, warned: **"There is no retreat but in submission and slavery! Our chains are forged. . . Is life so dear, or peace so sweet, as to be purchased at the price of chains and slavery? Forbid it, Almighty God! I know not what course others may take; but as for me: Give me Liberty, or Give me Death!"** [81]

With grave concern Thomas Jefferson and fifty-five other fearless men drew up and signed a Declaration of Independence. This was no superficial or thoughtless decision, for every man knew it meant either freedom or death: There was no neutral ground. The possibility of being hanged as traitors loomed large. They saw no other option. It was indeed a solemn meeting as each man took the quill and signed his name. John Hancock, the first to sign the Document, did so with a large signature to let the King know of his commitment. Having lost a ship for non-payment of taxes, and with a price on his head, Hancock broke the solemn silence after each man had signed, saying: **"Gentlemen: The price on my head has just been doubled!"**[82]

Samuel Adams, the firebrand of the Revolution, saw his life's main work come to a head with the signing of the Declaration of Independence. He had organized the Committee of Correspondence, which was instrumental in uniting the Colonies into a cohesive and agreeable unit. Without telegraph, television or radio, this was a tremendous task to coordinate thinking and activities relating to the Revolution. If we could name one city as the birthplace of the Revolution it would be Boston: It was there that the Sons of Liberty were organized in 1765 [due to the Stamp Act], and by the end of the year that organization existed in all thirteen colonies. Eight years later, in 1773, it was Sam Adams and the Sons of Liberty that took to throwing almost two million dollars worth of British Tea into the Harbor. Now, it was July 2, 1776, and Sam Adams could hardly contain his joy: This, the signing of the Declaration of Independence was the culmination of his efforts. Adams' exalted view of Christianity is refreshing. He declared: **"The Bible carries with it the history of the creation, the fall and redemption of man, and discloses to him, in the infant born at Bethlehem, the Legislator and Savior of the world."**[83] The Signers of the Declaration were soon joined by an increasing number of Americans in the battle for Liberty. Many, including John Adams, were convinced that they were actually ushering in the Kingdom of Jesus Christ. We dare not fault them for this. Jonathan Edwards himself leaned that direction; the dramatic social changes that took place in America since the Great Awakening, and the peaceful times under the Constitution urged on that kind of excitement and joy.

As people heard of the signing of a Declaration of Independence, elated joy spread across the land.

There was cheering, waving, the ringing of church bells and the wasting of left-over gunpowder. Samuel Adams said the people recognized the resolution as a decree from heaven, for it was: The formerly dry bones had become a living, breathing mighty army.

When the battle for Independence was over, John Hancock revealed the important connection between Christianity and the Constitution. He said: **"Let an association be formed to be denominated 'The Christian Constitutional Society,' it's object to be first: The support of the Christian religion, second: The support of the United States."**[84]

M.E. Bradford noted that **"with no more than five exceptions"** the Signers of the Declaration of Independence were **"all members of one of the established Christian communions."**[85] While that does not reveal if they were born-again believers, it does mean they understood that man was inwardly depraved and in need of a Savior. Perhaps the most noteworthy personal quality of the Founders was their humility, a humility attributed to their thoughts of God and the Christianity that prompted those thoughts. Anyone who is aware of his own inward depravity, and his personal need of a Savior, will not be haughty toward God or arrogant toward his fellowman. And, he will also be happier with a God over him!

One of the members of the "mighty army" worth mentioning is General Nathanael Greene [1742-1786], the son of a Quaker farmer. He was so respected by General George Washington from the very first time they met, that Washington elevated him to Brigadier

General. His effective tactics throughout the War [April 19, 1775 – April 11, 1783] deserves praise. Because of his maneuvers the war continually turned in the favor of the Colonies. His genuine Christian attitude was a blessing to all who knew him, and his humble demeanor toward the Lord might well have been the reason why the Hand of Providence rested upon him and his military wisdom. General Washington had decided that, in the event of his own death, Greene would take his place. Of all the officers who fought in the War, only Washington and Greene served throughout the entire eight years.

Independence! A Nation in which the people ruled; where elected officials were actually servants of the people! No other nation on earth had ever been placed on such a Foundation. This would require every citizen to be self-governed, well in control of their lives and responsible for their attitudes and actions. Independence for the individual! That is, they would be free from all outside controls in their lives. And Independence for the nation! Which means no other nation would be in command of any American affairs.

President George Washington understood! He touched on many things in his Farewell Address: Two of them deserve our attention because they deal with Independence. First, he warned the day may come when **"unprincipled men will be enabled to subvert the power of the people, and to usurp for themselves the reins of government . . ."** If that happens, We The People will no longer be Independent and Free; we will be the slaves and the

Government will be free to do whatever it pleases with us. Second, Washington had a word regarding unhealthy alliances with other nations saying, **"The nation which indulges toward another an habitual hatred or an habitual fondness is in some degree a slave. It is a slave to its animosity or to its affection, either of which is sufficient to lead it astray from its duty and its interest."**[86] President Washington laid out this principle clearly, which is fitting for the Nation as well as extremely advisable for every individual who expects to enjoy personal Independence.

American Independence came out of the Great Awakening! It was in the very heart of God that man should be independent. The Christian should never think, however, that he can become independent of Jesus Christ. John tells us: *"He who has the Son has life; he who does not have the Son of God does not have life."* [1 John 5:12] The Christian is never independent of Him; for *"in Him we live and move and exist . . . for we are His offspring."* [Acts 17:28]

10 – LIBERTY: A VITAL INGREDIENT

To fully appreciate the magnitude of the Great Awakening one would have to be there: It is an experience to be experienced, not merely analyzed and discussed. Those who know not the Lord will either reject the Awakening outright or lay it to an emotional fervor generated by men who knew how to manipulate crowds. But the evidence is in: Hearts were changed by the intense presence of God, and men were brought to a joyous loyalty to Jesus Christ, The Church proceeded to love and minister as Jesus Christ did while on earth. Men not only became solid church members; they were also faithful neighbors and respected citizens.

Over and above the personal lives that were changed, the whole of society was altered and prepared for the Battle for Independence that began at Lexington Green. The following excerpts from **Paul Revere's Ride,** authored by Henry Wadsworth Longfellow, America's Poet, describes what happened:

Listen, my children, and you shall hear
Of the midnight ride of Paul Revere:
On the eighteenth of April, in Seventy-five;
Hardly a man is now alive
Who remembers that famous day and year!

He said to his friend, "If the British march
By land or sea from the town to-night,
Hang a lantern aloft in the belfry arch
Of the North Church tower as a signal light—

One if by land, and two, if by sea;
And I on the opposite shore will be
Ready to ride and spread the alarm
Through every Middlesex village and farm
For the country folk to be up and to arm."

Then he climbed the tower of the Old North
    Church,
By the wooden stairs, with stealthy tread,
To the belfry-chamber overhead,
And startled the pigeons on their perch
By the trembling ladder, steep and tall
To the highest window in the wall;
Where he paused to listen and look down
A moment on the roofs of the town,
And the moonlight flowing over all.

Meanwhile, impatient to mount and ride,
Booted and spurred, with a heavy stride;
And lo! As he looks on the belfry's height
A glimmer, and then a gleam of light!
He springs to the saddle, the bridle he turns,
But lingers and gazes, till full on his sight
A second lamp in the belfry burns!

A hurry of hoofs in a village street,
A shape in the moonlight, a bulk in the dark.
And beneath, from the pebble, in passing, a
    spark
Struck out by a stead flying fearless and fleet;
That was all! And yet, through the gloom and the
    light,

The fate of a nation was riding that night.
And the spark struck out by the stead in his
    flight
Kindled the land into flame with the heat.

You know the rest. In the books you have read
How the British Regulars fired and fled—
How the farmers gave them ball for ball,
From behind each fence and farm-yard wall,
Chasing the red-coats down the lane
Then crossing the fields to emerge again;
Under the trees at the turn of the road,
And only pausing to fire and load.

So through the night rode Paul Revere;
And so through the night went his cry of alarm
To every Middlesex village and farm—
A cry of defiance and not of fear,
A voice in the darkness, a knock at the door,
And a word that shall echo forevermore!
For, borne on the night-wind of the Past,
Through all our history, to the last,
In the hour of darkness and peril and need,
The people will waken and listen and hear
The hurrying hoof-beats of that stead,
And the midnight message of Paul Revere.[87]

"The people will waken and listen and hear!"
Longfellow confidently tells us! Will these bones
live again? Will America hear? If America was to
be an instrument for good in the hand of God she
must first break off all other loyalties. This event on

the 18th of April in 1775 was simply a result of the inward freedom Americans had inherited at the time of the Great Awakening: They were now competent to handle national freedom! If the Colonists had not known inner freedom, if the **"dry bones"** were still spiritually lifeless, America would only have contended for selfish interests, not the safety and benefit of their children, and their children's children.

William Penn [1644-1718] is a noble result of the persuasive winds of God. As a teen he was a renegade, the son of an Admiral in the British Navy. Then he was converted to faith in Jesus Christ; and at the young age of 26, Penn was pastor of a Quaker Church in England. On Sunday, August 14, 1670, when he and his Assistant Pastor William Mead, arrived at their church building, he found the sheriff had padlocked the doors. So he and his 300 or so parishioners worshipped in the street – for which Penn and Mead were imprisoned! He had violated a conventicle law that prohibited church meetings without permission from the Church of England. When brought to trial, the jury, headed by Edward Bushel, found Penn and Mead not guilty. The Court ordered the jury to reconsider, but they came back with a similar verdict. The third time the judge ordered them sequestered over night, without provisions or a chamber pot. They returned to the courtroom the next morning hungry and in an odorous condition, but they again returned a similar verdict. The judge was furious: He had no option but to release Penn and Mead, but he imprisoned the twelve jury members for disobeying his orders. A heavy fine was assessed against each jury member: Some paid, but Mr. Bushel and three others stayed in jail until an elderly judge came out of retirement two months later to review the case and clear up the injustice.

William Penn's father had been an Admiral in the King's Navy. When he died, the King of England owed him a sizeable sum. To settle the estate of the Senior Penn, the King gave young William a piece of land in America. It came to be called Pennsylvania. The first legislative act of Pennsylvania on April 25, 1682, read: **"Whereas the glory of Almighty God and the good of mankind is the reason and the end of government, and, therefore government itself is a venerable ordinance of God. . . [there shall be established] laws as shall best preserve true Christian and civil liberty, in opposition to all unchristian, licentious, and unjust practices, whereby God may have his due, and Caesar his due, and the people their due, from tyranny and oppression."[88]**

This first act defines for us **"true Christian and civil liberty,"** which resulted in freedom from **"tyranny and oppression."** Pennsylvania for many years was a grand demonstration of religious liberty. William Penn wrote a letter to Peter the Great, Czar of Russia, in which he said that **"If thou wouldst rule well, thou must rule for God, and to do that, thou must be ruled by Him. Those who will not be governed by God will be ruled by tyrants."[89]**

Liberty did not mean the freedom to fulfill the lusts of the flesh. In 1815, the Supreme Court of

Pennsylvania dealt with a case where a lewd picture [apparently pornography of some sort] was displayed in a private room to those who paid a fee for the privilege of viewing. Six men were found guilty: The Court said: **"The corruption of the public mind, in general, and debauching the manners of youth, in particular, by lewd and obscene pictures exhibited to view, must necessarily be attended with the most injurious consequences. . . No man is permitted to corrupt the morals of the people; secret poison cannot be thus disseminated."[90]**

That Pennsylvania case was in 1815! William Penn's conversion 150 years earlier, and the Great Awakening 85 years earlier, still had a great affect on the moral climate of Pennsylvania. Today, Pennsylvania is like all other states, having lost sight of its moral foundation and purpose – **the glory of Almighty God**. No city, state or nation can expect to have a good culture while offending Jesus Christ.

The people of Philadelphia, the people of America, almost to a man, tell us that Liberty is the freedom to do whatever I want to do. A 2008 TV ad has a woman saying: **"Freedom means I can say whatever I want to say, when I want to say it!"** That is not Biblical Freedom. True Freedom is being liberated from sin so as to please God! It is being freed from the impulse to say and do whatever I want, when I want.

The intense presence of God swept the Colonies in the 1740s and prepared early men and women for the founding of a new nation under God: It was to remain a nation under God. To the Colonists Liberty meant freedom from anything that kept them from pleasing Jesus Christ. That meant freedom from [1] British tyranny, [2] Roman dominion, [3] the paganism of the French Enlightenment and [4] the inner compulsion to selfishness and sin. All elements of their lives were to be brought under the authority of Jesus Christ and His Cross. That is Liberty—the one vital ingredient in any successful nation!

It remains forever true: ***"Blessed is the nation whose God is the Lord!"*** [Psalm 33:12]

11 – WISDOM OF THE FATHERS

America is living in a youth-dominated culture. This crafts a serious problem – it ignores the counsel of fathers! In Greek culture, wisdom dwells with the youth; in Hebrew culture wisdom is found with fathers. Inasmuch as our culture is based on the Hebrew/Christian model, we take pleasure and delight in the wisdom that comes to us through our American forefathers.

The Federalist Papers, written by Alexander Hamilton, James Madison and John Jay, is a series of articles that appeared from time to time in New York City newspapers. These articles were written in 1787 and 1788, and were designed to educate America on the value of the new Constitution recently adopted. Every family should have a copy of **The Federalist Papers**, even if not read word-for-word: It will serve as a great reference book. For example, James Madison said in **The Federalist Papers**: **"It is impossible for the man of pious reflection not to perceive in [the Constitution] a finger of that Almighty hand which has been so frequently and signally extended to our relief in the critical stages of the revolution."**[91]Oh, if Americans could only sense what Madison sensed – the finger of God's Almighty Hand!

Here we face serious questions: What did the Almighty Hand have to do with our Constitution? What effect would the life of Jesus, who lived eighteen hundred years ago, have upon their deliberations and their new country? Was the life of Jesus simply used by the Founders for their own political ends? Did they need a Christian philosophy that would justify a revolution? Why not an Eastern religion or Roman Catholicism or Judaism or Islam or the Church of England, or paganism? Was Christianity the actual foundation for this new nation or merely a good psychological prop? Was there indeed an **"Invisible Hand which conducts the affairs of men,"** as George Washington stated in his Inaugural Address, April 30, 1789?

To be sure – God is not mocked! He will not allow Christianity and His Son to be used for selfish ends. The Founders knew this; they were convinced that without that Invisible Hand they had no hope for success. Perhaps there is more to the Christian religion than being merely a wing of a political party.

Consider Christianity as it weaves its way through the life of Noah Webster [1758-1843], a man who quietly served in the background of the American Revolution. He was a man who can rightly be called one of our Forefathers, though he was only 18-years old at the signing of the Declaration of Independence. Of all the Founders, George Washington was the most illustrious and vital to America's success. He had been Providentially raised and preserved for such a time as this! A multitude might come in second, including Noah Webster, though he signed neither the Declaration nor the U.S. Constitution. His influence was beyond measure. The world knows of his crowning work, his **1828 Dictionary of the English Language**. Few realize he was the

Founding Father of American Scholarship and Education. Webster, perhaps more than any other, kept Christianity and Education indivisibly united. He had installed Christianity as the foundation of American Education. When John Dewey [1859-1952], the secular humanist, came on the scene he removed all reference to God and Christianity from America's educational system. Noah Webster's prime concern was for the welfare of the youth. He believed they should be taught self-government, and that the principles of republican government have their origin in the Scriptures. Consequently, he sought to build an educational system embodying a love of virtue, patriotism, and religion. Webster believed that, in order to instill self-government in the lives of the young people of America, the Bible furnished all necessary rules to direct our conduct, adding that, **"No truth is more evident to my mind than that the Christian religion must be the basis of any government intended to secure the rights and privileges of a free people ... When I speak of the Christian religion as the basis of government, I do not mean an ecclesiastical establishment, a creed, or rites, forms, and ceremonies. I mean primitive Christianity . . . as taught by Christ and His apostles . . . consisting in a belief in the moral government of God . . ."**[92] Webster gave himself to this end! He did not see Christianity as the best foundation: It was the ONLY foundation, for it was from God Himself! It was this dedication that prompted him to prepare his dictionary – which he put in order by himself in the following manner:

On a large circular table, with an open center, were placed twenty to thirty foreign language dictionaries. Webster, from the center of this table, moved from one dictionary to the next as he settled on the meaning of each word, recorded the definition in his **Dictionary** when he was satisfied with the exact meaning; then he moved on to the next word.

Dictionaries in use today are changing constantly: As soon as a new word is used by society, be it vulgar, crude or worthless, it quickly finds its way into the dictionary. Webster, on the other hand, purposefully omitted the vulgarities of Europe, keeping American English pure for the benefit of educating the youth. This Dictionary proved spiritually constructive for many years.

At the time of the Constitutional Convention in Philadelphia, Noah Webster was a 29-year old school master. He was visited by many of the outstanding delegates. They came to his home where they discussed strategy and policy and how Christianity related to this new nation. Among the many visitors were George Washington, Benjamin Franklin, James Madison, Edmund Randolph, Roger Sherman, William Livingston and John Marshall and many others.

Although he classified himself as a Christian through his early years – for he believed in the Bible – it was not until he was forty-nine that he found peace and assurance of his salvation. He had been impressed with the precepts of Christianity, but now he had come to personal faith and joy. It happened this way: His wife and especially his two eldest daughters had attended a revival and were greatly moved. That was in 1807. Webster himself resisted the invites of his daughters, but finally agreed to go and was touched by the genuine nature of those who attended. He was soon led by a spontaneous impulse to repent, pray, and entirely surrender to Jesus Christ, his Maker and Redeemer. His submission was cheerful and, he states, it **"was followed by the peace of mind which the world can neither give nor take away."**[93]

Webster finished his Dictionary and had it published when he was 70-years old. Four years later he published his **History of the United States**. He was the first to introduce the study of American History into school textbooks. In his writings he traced the Hand of God in western history, while also evidencing the relationship of America to the Bible.

Noah Webster's studies centered in language and words! He was convinced that a national language provides national unity. He had a single goal in his life of ninety-three years – to see youth educated to be wise and virtuous. His definition of Education tells us that **education comprehends all that series of instruction and discipline which is intended to enlighten the understanding, correct the temper, and form the manners and habits of youth, and fit them for usefulness in their future stations. To give children a good education in manners, arts and science, is important; to give them a religious education is indispensable; and an immense responsibility rests on parents and guardians who neglect these duties.** The wisdom of this insightful

Forefather would go a long way to correct the vulgar and valueless goals of our secular education today!

Another man worth considering is John Dickinson. He was intellectually brilliant beyond many, was a serious Christian, a loyal companion in this new Republic and perhaps the most underrated Founder of this country.

Dickinson, a delegate to the Constitutional Convention from Delaware, had strong Quaker leanings, having been raised in that Church. The Quakers do not believe in war. So he opposed the Declaration of Independence until and unless a national government had been created and foreign assistance obtained. [It sounds like he would approve of the UN!] But there is more: Dickinson was overruled, for the rest of the delegates saw Independence justified under the Law of Nature without waiting for foreign approval. [Good point!] Dickinson, rather than voting against Independence, voluntarily abstained so the vote would be unanimous. Then, as soon as the Convention was over he immediately departed for military service. Such was his Christian loyalty to the cause of Liberty. Dickinson's Christianity also prompted him to free the slaves he inherited from his father, and in the convention he sought to prevent the Constitution from encouraging slavery in any way. His eloquence, both in speech and on paper, was unsurpassed. For Dickinson, Liberty not only meant Liberty for himself; it also meant Liberty from England and Liberty for slaves. It would take another seventy years before Abraham Lincoln would issue his **<u>Emancipation Proclamation</u>**.

That which made the Forefathers spiritual giants was their spiritual conversion. They had a personal relationship with God. It was not warm and fuzzy, but it did instill responsibility to God and loyalty in their human relations. Out of this flowed the Declaration of Independence wherein they **pledged to each other their Lives, their Fortunes and their sacred Honor.**

The bottom line in their relations with God was that Jesus Christ had died for them, suffering an unbearable punishment for an unbelievable crime, taking the guilt upon Him and bearing it on the Cross. Dietrich Bonhoeffer explains: **"Behold the God who has become man, the unfathomable mystery of the love of God for the world. God loves man. It is not an ideal man that He loves, but man as he is. What we find abominable is man's opposition to God . . . This is for God the ground for unfathomable love. A love which left man alone in his guilt would not be love. From His selfless love, from His freedom from sin, Jesus enters into the guilt of men and takes this guilt upon Himself."**[94] This was basic in their personal as well as their corporate lives.

History records the testimonies of a number of our Founders, men who came to faith in Jesus Christ. Of all the Founders, George Washington was the most impressive! Looking at the exterior we see one who is tall, competent, self-controlled and politically astute. But that which made him impressive was his personal relationship with Jesus Christ: Early in his life he came to believe in the blood of Jesus Christ for the cleansing of his life from sin. Henry

Muhlenberg, pastor of a Lutheran church near Valley Forge, PA., and one of the founders of the Lutheran Church in America, said that **"George Washington rode around among his army yesterday and admonished each and every one to fear God, to put away the wickedness that has set in and become so general, and to practice the Christian virtues. . . . [Washington] respects God's Word, believes in the atonement through Christ, and bears himself in humility and gentleness. Therefore, the Lord God . . . has hitherto graciously held him in His hand as a chosen vessel."[95]**

For the signers, generally speaking, the Declaration of Independence was a personal venture with God, not merely a human endeavor. It would not be an automatic victory, however, for some of the signers would lose their homes, their businesses, and some their lives. After the struggle for Independence was over, none would say it cost too much – except the British! Our Forefathers sensed the God of Providence was personally involved from beginning to end.

We must mention one more patriot, Patrick Henry [1736-1799]. His speech before the Virginia House, a full year before the signing of the Declaration of Independence, re-echoed the words of Pastor Baldwin in Danbury, Connecticut, quoted above. Henry asked the delegates: **"Is life so dear, or peace so sweet, as to be purchased at the price of chains and slavery?"[96]** Those who knew Patrick Henry and those who have read details of his life knew of his Christian faith and personal walk with Jesus Christ:

He said: **"It cannot be emphasized too strongly or too often that this great nation was founded, not by religionists, but by Christians, not on religions, but on the Gospel of Jesus Christ."** [97]

The Gospel of Jesus Christ! That was the Gospel that came through the Apostle Paul and called him to go to Macedonia. From there the Word went to Rome and on to Germany and Europe, England and came ultimately to America. The early Colonists sensed they were a part of God's intention for the Gospel of Jesus Christ to flow from these shores to the nations and islands of the world. Since the early days of America, thousands of missionaries have taken the message of Jesus Christ to every continent. Without the Great Awakening, any nation that might develop would be stagnant; missions would have been lifeless. Consider the millions in Africa, as well as the additional multitudes in present-day China who are coming to faith in Jesus Christ. This working of God's Spirit can be traced to America's Great Awakening. The Spirit who opened the hearts of the Colonists prior to the founding of this great nation continues to open hearts to the Gospel of Jesus Christ all over the globe.

The Founders were men of God; not mere puppets whose strings were pulled by religious charlatans. These men knew Jesus and became His loyal followers, for it was Jesus Christ who had breathed life into them when they were but dry bones – as Paul told Ephesian believers: **"You were dead in your trespasses and sins. But God, who is rich in mercy, because of His great love with which He** loves us, when we were dead in sin, made us alive together with Christ – for by grace you are saved. For by grace you have been saved through faith; and that not of yourself. It is the gift of God . . . lest any man should boast." [Eph.2:1, 4-5, 8-9]

Can these bones live again? How much do we want them to live again, become a mighty army? God's promise remains: **"You will find Me when you search for Me with all your heart!"** [Jeremiah 29:13]

12 – A LIFE OF MISERY AND MIRACLES [98]

The Great Awakening had undeniable effects on the American culture. And the greatest effect was the Revolution. In the final analysis we must conclude that the American Revolution was the plan of God Himself – which began in the Great Awakening! Yes! These bones can live! Observe what the Awakening brought: Independence; a new nation; a Constitution; the expanse of trade; newly guaranteed Freedoms; the Bill of Rights; the absence of British troops in American homes, American-chosen legislators and judges, trial by jury, a righteous and congenial culture, unlimited publication of Bibles and much, much, much more. There were also uncomfortable side effects: Consider the case of Mary Young, one of many stories to be told.

Around 1770, teen-ager Mary Young left Germany with her parents, Jacob and Maria and her two brothers, Jacob and John. They sailed to America to start a new farm life, but tragedy struck on the high seas: Both of her parents died; then one brother and then the other also died due to foul living quarters on board. Mary was overwhelmed with grief – and she was all alone. A young man by the name of Theodore Benz, sensing her pain, introduced himself. He had left Germany alone because his parents did not have the funds to come at this time. Theodore and Mary became close friends. When they arrived in Philadelphia they were greeted by Henry Muhlenberg, the local Lutheran pastor. [Henry was the father of Peter Muhlenberg, the Virginia preacher mentioned in an earlier chapter].

The population of Philadelphia in 1770 was 16,000, plus 4,000 British troops. Soon Pastor Henry lined up Theodore as a hired man on Mr. Leinbach's farm near Oley, Pennsylvania. Mary stayed in Philadelphia some sixty miles away, working for Mary Kreider. Farmer Leinbach was so impressed with the help he received from Theodore during the first year that he deeded over a choice piece of land for him and Mary, his bride-to-be. Theodore could hardly wait to ride his horse into town to tell Mary the news. While there he heard of the need for volunteers in the War for Independence. Theodore's friends were joining, and he reasoned in his heart, **"What good is the farm to Mary and me if the British win?"** With fear, yet without hesitation, Theodore sensed it was his duty to join General Washington's army!

Hurriedly, arrangements were made for a wedding. Theodore wanted Mary to have a nice farm on which to live if something should happen to him. After the wedding, and after hugs and tears, Theodore with others from the Philadelphia area marched off to war.

Amid a stormy battle in which many were killed, wounded or captured, Theodore's friends lost sight of him. Perhaps he was on a British prison ship or in some hospital. Search was made, but as days wore on into weeks, and then months, all hope expired: Theodore was never found.

The loss of Theodore was devastating for Mary. She had lost both her whole family at sea – and now her beloved Theodore. She grew pale and emaciated, as well as inconsolable. Her grief seemed more than she could live with. Friends helped construct a house for her on her farm near Oley, a home where she could live out her days in quiet solitude. She never re-married.

As Mary walked around her farm she discovered something: Many valuable herbs that could be used as medicines. Her herbs made her acquainted with the sick people in the area and beyond, many coming from as far away as 400 miles to share in her healing finds. She came to be known as *"Mountain Mary."* What her herbs could not cure, her compassionate nursing often did. Many times she watched at the sick bed of the dying with Gospel comfort. Mary had found peace with God and with her circumstances. She who had been comforted by the Spirit of God in her time of grief had come to know how to minister healing and comfort to others. For more than thirty years she healed sick bodies and comforted troubled souls, walking contentedly in the path that Providence had laid out for her.

Mary died in 1819 and her funeral was held in her adopted town. No funeral in Oley carried with it the grandeur and dignity of this one. Every home in Oley was represented. People came in wagons and on horseback from far and wide. Many of those who came had savored her kindness in life. Now, with few dry eyes in the assembly, they gave her due respects as she exchanged the things that are seen for those things God has prepared for them that love Him.

This account of Mary and Theodore is only a small picture of the many who suffered that we might know Liberty. Mary lost all those she knew and loved, but out of that loss she found a reality in Christ Jesus that produced a blessing for the world. Would Mary have ordered her life differently? Of course! But was she satisfied with the way God had order it? Of course! And so were the hundreds who were blessed by her life.[98]

SECTION III –

SPINELESS REASONING

W hen the human body ages its capacities diminish! The heart slows; breathing is labored; the digestive system – and the brain – needs vitamin assistance; the reproductive system fails; diseases cannot be easily resisted; eventually the heart stops. Such is the routine as man returns to the dust from whence he came. But need this be so in the life of a nation – especially if that nation seeks to walk in the ways of God? Are there leaders – perhaps a Pastor – who will show us those ways?

As the Pastor goes, so goes the Church, so goes society, so goes the nation! God's desire is that someone would step forward and set the course for society. The one qualified to do this is the born-again Christian; the one changed by the indwelling Spirit. And the one best qualified is he who has been given a sacred desk to stand behind from Sunday after Sunday, anointed to present the Word of God!

Lamentably, such is not always the case. There are an increasing number of defections from the pulpit; there is also a growing fascination with psychology, philosophy, mysticism, materialism, motivationalism and false religions. The Supreme Court combs the world in the hope of finding better laws than those in the U.S. Constitution; in the same manner too many pastors comb the world in the hope of finding Truth that might be better than the Truth they had found in Christian Scripture.

This Section is primarily addressed to the pulpit, but applies to us all! It is written to create a spiritual awareness in each of us, not to snub or criticize the under-shepherd but to hold him up for God's blessing and protection from the enemy's distractions, enticements and discouragements. May the Church – beginning with the pulpit – experience again the breath of God!

"Beloved . . . sternly contend for the faith which was once for all delivered to the saints. For certain persons have crept in unaware – who turn the grace of God into self-indulgence, denying the Lordship of our Master, Jesus Christ." [Jude, Vs.3-4]

The Colonial Church had a strong Backbone: Its pulpit was most concerned with doctrinal purity. Bonhoeffer write: **"False doctrine corrupts the life of the Church at its source, and that is why doctrinal sin is more serious than moral. Those who rob the Church of the Gospel deserve the**

ultimate penalty, whereas those who fail in morality have the Gospel there to help them."[99] Comparing present-day America with the original Backbone, we sadly watch the Glory fade and die.

There is a growing apathy in America, a growing rebellion but a deepening concern in the hearts of those who hunger for righteousness and reality in Jesus Christ: The latter have a genuine desire for His will to be **done on earth as it is in heaven** [Matthew 6:10].

It was not long after the founding of our country that folks could no longer explain our successful revolution to the world or even to ourselves, so states Dr. Irving Kristol, [the father of Bill Kristol of **The Weekly Standard**.][100] Those who were thinking men had turned away from politics. Political thought had lost its vigor, Kristol tells us. We today have long forgotten the bondage under the Church of England, the corrupt culture of Europe, the Great Awakening, the separation of our culture from that of the Old Country, the declaring of independence from Britain and the signing of a new Constitution! We have even forgotten that America's success as a nation, and her achievements in industry, commerce and transportation was and is a result of our "escape" from the past. We have also forgotten – or never knew it in the first place – that the Hand of Providence brought it all about!

There are major issues before us with society now embracing secular humanism, evolution and a self-centered approach to life, a self-centered approach that is fast becoming the core of the Church, a Church that does little to counteract society's foolishness. In addition, many foreign elements are being embraced by the Church. In the light of three centuries of Providential care over this country, and the tremendous potential in Jesus Christ only, will there be a shaking and a coming together of the dry bones one more time before He returns? Or, will the Church be satisfied – like the five foolish virgins – to sleep until He comes? [See Matthew 25:1-13]

13 – EDUCATION: SLIDING INTO THE VOID

We teach our students what we know –more or less! The spiritual teacher conveys something the humanist cannot, for he transmits spirit and life with the words he teaches. The humanist delivers doubts, questions and uncertainties with the information he gives students. One is creative; the other destructive!

Education in early America was simple. The Pastor, whether a graduate of Harvard or Yale, was qualified to preach from the pulpit or teach in the classroom! The Christian education of the community was his objective in either case. His Sunday message – sometimes three to four hours long – might include lessons in civics, history, morality, relationships, Providence, rights and revolution. The final duty on the education of children rested with parents. The goal of education, by parent or pastor, was twofold: To assist the student in establishing a relationship with God and to teach the student how to live in the new republic. In both of these endeavors the Bible was essential. Present-day education has deleted God from the mix: As a result the school system has an impossible task for, without God, who is to say any action toward fellow men is right or wrong? The field of Ethics is empty, as is psychology, philosophy and the humanities.

Consider the theory of education proposed by John Dewey [1859-1952], who said man is devoid of spirit. And, he tells us, if the environment is good, man will be good: Thus it is mandatory for society to provide a good environment. This served – and still serves – as the basic foundation for liberalism. Dewey also said the primary goal of schools was to "socialize" the student.[100]

William H. McGuffy [1800-1873] was of the old school, and would not have agreed with Dewey. McGuffey was still a partaker of the Colonial spirit. He was a roving teacher at the age of 14, with 48 students in one classroom. This was no small task when you realize his students ranged from age six to twenty-one. Students brought their own books, primarily the Bible since few other textbooks existed. In 1836 McGuffey developed several Eclectic Readers, duly graded for various ages. Here is one excerpt from *Lesson XXXI* in *Eclectic First Reader* entitled *Good Advice*

> **If you have done anything during the day that is wrong, ask forgiveness of God and your parents.**
> **If anyone has done you wrong, forgive him in your heart before you go to sleep. Do not go to sleep with hatred in your heart toward anyone.**
> **Never speak to anyone in an angry or harsh voice.**
> **If you have spoken unkind words to a brother or sister, go and ask forgiveness. If you have disobeyed your parents, go and confess it.**

Ask God to aid you always to do good and avoid evil.[101]

Henry Ford [1863-1947], founder of the Ford Motor Company, was an avid fan of McGuffey's Readers, and considered them his Alma Mater. McGuffey's Readers had a prominent place in education in the 1800s.

How things have changed! America's current educational dilemma began with the influx of modern psychology into the educational system. This originated with Professor Wilhelm M. Wundt [1832-1920], of the University of Leipzig in Germany, who studied the student's **"psyche."** John Dewey [1859-1952], one of the founders of the American Humanist Association, and considered to be the Father of American Progressive Education, stated that, **"There is no God and there is no soul. Hence, there is no need for the props of traditional religion. With dogma and creed excluded, the immutable truth is also dead and buried. There is no room for fixed, natural law or moral absolutes.**[102]

Dewey's thinking originated with Wilhelm Wundt who believed a child was a mere animal upon which the teacher was to project stimuli. John Dewey accepted the same premise. Both Wundt and Dewey relied on Evolution; the results of this are seen in children accepting that concept and living out their natural instincts. McGuffy instilled self-discipline in his students; Dewey went for self-expression and unbridled actions

Professor Wundt's first American student, G. Stanley Hall [1844-1924], along with John Dewey, adopted the following theories and implemented them in American education:

1 – Man is devoid of spirit.
2 – Man is good when the environment is good; so the duty of society is to provide a good environment.
3 – A student is not a reasoning being, but an entity upon which a teacher projects stimuli.
4 – The primary goal of schools it to "socialize" the student.
5 – Schools became laboratories where students are studied by teachers to see **how** they learned. **What** they learned is secondary!
6 – Education developed followers, not a society of people with God-given capacity for leadership. [103]

Dewey's concepts became the basis upon which Louis Raths formed his Values-Clarification scheme. Dewey believed that, in the absence of a Supreme God, the child is sufficient in and of himself to formulate ethical choices. **Values Clarification** by Simon, Howe and Kirschenbaum, is a 397-page handbook for teachers and students, and is based on Raths' approach. This book **Is not concerned with the content of people's values, but the process of valuing.** In order to help students clarify their values, seventy-nine strategy sessions are outlined in the book. Following are typical questions:

Strategy Number 4: Which do you think is the worst?

_____ to become pregnant
_____ to be dependent upon hard drugs
_____ to date someone from another race

Strategy Number 21: To whom would you tell?

_____ you have had premarital sex
_____ you cheat on your income tax
_____ you have considered suicide
_____ you have had an abortion
_____ you have doubts about religion
_____ your method of birth control

In the above scheme of things, the teacher is not to assist or assess the decision. In fact, any and all decisions are right. There are no absolutes. Education today attempts to develop the innate goodness and wisdom already residing in the student! Noah Webster, on the other hand, saw education as imparting character and virtue from the teacher to the student. Today we trust in the wisdom of the student, the teacher being a facilitator who attempts to find some wisdom in the immature mind. On the other hand, our Forefathers, including Webster and McGuffy, knew that God's wisdom and virtue is to be conveyed through a godly teacher.

To understand the discrepancy between Colonial education and modern education we start with the

Bible, the Standard by which all things are rightly measured. The Bible was the Colonial textbook, but is excluded from today's classroom. As we examine it further we see that the Bible teaches that Adam and Eve committed the original sin, and that sin has been passed on to all mankind. John Dewey and humanist educators may deny this; but the denial cannot change the truth regarding our original parents. Secular liberals want the Bible's record of Adam and Eve and original sin expunged from modern education, pressing for the separation of church and state. However, what did it do to our children? It deprived them of the truth! If truth is not the prime concern of the educational establishment, what is their chief concern?

When Dewey's concepts removed God, Jesus Christ and the Bible from the classroom, it became necessary to deal with little Johnnie's problems in school in a humanistic way, without reference to ultimate reality. If there is no God – as Dewey claims – there is no sin! Without sin man is considered neutral or essentially good. Thus, teachers and school administrators have neither an explanation for the troubles and crimes in students' hearts, nor do they have a solution. The best that can be done is cut the classroom size, pay the teachers more, add psychiatrists, psychoanalysts and counselors to the payroll and hurl more money at the problem. Educational costs multiply – but so do disciplinary problems!

The Principle Approach to Education is simple: Instead of granting an external, physical or even a psychological reward for completing a task, the Principle approach sees the completion of the task or lesson as reward in and of itself.

Educator Rosalie Slater tells us: **"The battle today is for men's hearts and souls. It is not a battle for men's minds. The mind will believe only what the heart, the character, the conscience, of an individual dictates."**[104]

The Conscience condemns or approves an action based on a pre-established standard. A student whose standard is: *No Cheating,* is condemned when he finds his eyes wandering over to another's answers during a test. On the other hand, a student whose standard is: *Cheating is Sometimes Okay* feels satisfied when his eyes wander. Louis Raths and John Dewey would tell us that it is more important for the student to do the deciding than it is for him to decide correctly. That is troublesome for the student, for it shipwrecks his conscience on the shores of secular humanism. Anything is approved in the secular humanist's world as long as the student arrives at the decision without the influence of stodgy parents or a Christian teacher. On the other hand, the influence of an atheist or naturalist is heartily welcomed. Why? Because the atheist will not inject God into the student's world – the very thing the student needs.

We get a feel for true education and the development of Conscience as we read the following excerpts of a letter John Quincy Adams sent to his son George Washington Adams. It was written when Dad was in Russia on diplomatic business and young George was just ten-years old:

I advise you, my son, in whatever you read, and most of all in reading the Bible, to remember that it is for the purpose of making you wise and more virtuous. I have myself, for many years, made it a practice to read through the Bible once every year. I have always endeavored to read it with the same spirit and temper of mind, which I now recommend to you: that is, with the intention and desire that it may contribute to my advancement in wisdom and virtue.[105]

It is impossible to develop the Conscience aright without the Bible! Without a civil Conscience, that is, a Christian Conscience, society will revert to being savage. The evidence is in: We need look no further for proof than a comparison between our public schools today and the Colonial schools and homes. In those early homes no mention was directly made of the Principle Approach to education: However, in teaching the Bible the Principle Approach could not be avoided. Colonists knew of no other way to teach. A student learned correct arithmetic because of its intrinsic value, not because he got a star by his name. For the same reason he learned proper grammar, and proper penmanship. While grading of a student's work is important so that the student, teacher and parents can assess the student's progress – or lack thereof – grading is not a part of the Principle Approach where the student learns because of the essential worth of what is learned.

Not only is Conscience vital, so is Self-Government. When a student's Conscience is Biblically developed, he will be self-governed. Early

Americans knew Government was limited for it was unable to control the passions of the masses should they become rebellious or defiant. There was only one answer: SELF-Government – which is developed from the Bible. President John Adams said: **"Our Constitution was made only for a moral and religious people."** Adding, **"It is wholly inadequate for the government of any other."**[106]

Our Founders knew that godly Principles in the lives of citizens were vital to a healthy society. Pennsylvania had an effective way of dealing with criminals in early days: The incarcerated criminal was given a Bible and solitary confinement until he was *"penitent."* For this reason a prison was called a penitentiary.

Dr. Benjamin Rush [1745-1813] was a physician and signer of the Declaration of Independence. He was also the **"father of public schools"** and a leading promoter of the American Sunday School Union. He established the first free medical clinic and also founded the first anti-slavery society in America. Dr. Rush said: **"The only foundation for a republic is to be laid in religion. Without this there can be no virtue, and without virtue there can be no liberty, and liberty is the object and life of all republican government.** Rush also wrote: **The perfect morality of the Gospel rests upon . . . the vicarious life and death of the Son of God.**[107] It is not possible to be educated unto proper actions and attitudes without Christian Scriptures, the very thing rejected by the wise men of this world!

Preachers in Colonial America never worried about an ACLU-type lawsuit. They taught the Bible, knowing that Government, Society, the Church, and God, was on their side. Of course, they had no cause to fear for the whole culture had a Christian worldview, though not all were born again believers. There were none, however, to challenge the teaching of Biblical morals, the life and death of Jesus Christ, and forgiveness of sin through faith in Him. The teacher taught these truths and still had time to teach reading, writing and arithmetic, for spiritual lessons were incorporated in all academic studies. The student who was thus educated was morally upright and a good citizen; well equipped inwardly to live a self-governed life.

To be restored to what we should be – educationally, we must have things in their proper order. At the present it is impossible to simply change the laws, allowing the teaching of Creation, a respect for God and Jesus Christ, acknowledging a place for Bible study in public schools, a respect for the Flag and the Pledge of Allegiance, etc. Something else must take place first—and that is a general and Great Awakening of the citizenry to spiritual things. If there is no interest in spiritual things, any attempt to enforce spirituality through laws is useless. The present laws reflect what we are, our morals, attitudes and desires in life. The void we are drifting into is a godless void, adopted from France and the Enlightenment that exalted man above God.

The Great Awakening came before the Battle for Independence, before the Declaration of

Independence, before the Constitution, before the Bill of Rights. *"Lord Jesus Christ, in the midst of our confusion and lostness as a nation, send us another Great Awakening, for we have forgotten you, the Giver of every good and perfect gift, the Granter or our Inalienable Rights, the rightful Center of our culture. Give us insight to know where we are with You, so that we walk no more in darkness — for only in Thy Light do we see Light. Lord, breathe again on these dry bones!"*

14 – INDEPENDENCE WORTH FIGHTING FOR

Fifty-six men, on behalf of Thirteen Colonies, with the purpose of forming those Colonies into United States, wrote: **We hold these truths to be self-evident, that all men are created equal, that they are endowed by their Creator with certain unalienable Rights, that among these are Life, Liberty and the pursuit of Happiness. That, to secure these rights, Governments are instituted among Men, deriving their just powers from the consent of the governed. That whenever any Form of Government becomes destructive of these ends, it is the Right of the People to alter or to abolish it, and to institute new Government, laying its foundation on such principles and organizing its powers in such form, as to them shall seem most likely to effect their Safety and Happiness."** [Declaration of Independence]

There are five Self-Evident Truths in the Declaration, each starting with the word **That**. Here are the five:

That – all men are created equal.
That – it was the Creator who endowed men with certain inalienable Rights.
That – three of these Rights are: Life, Liberty and the pursuit of Happiness.
That – governments are instituted for this purpose: to secure inalienable Rights.

That – the people may change the Form of Government when that is in their best interest.

Americans now live in a postmodern world. That means, among many things, they reject absolutes, preferring to think in relative terms. It also means that we no longer read the Declaration of Independence in fixed and definite ways. One postmodern American recently said the self-evident truths in the Declaration may have been self-evident to them, but they are no longer self-evident to me. He apparently meant that if they are not self-evident to him they are no longer self-evident, nor are they of any value. The sole reason that Inalienable Rights and being Created Equal, etc, are self-evident to some and not to others has to do with Christianity: The Christian sees certain things that those who are not saved cannot see. Inalienable Rights were obvious – and self-evident – to those who had been spiritually awakened during and after the Great Awakening, as well as those who had studied the Law of Nature, Common Law, Blackstone and, of course, the Bible.

The truths referred to are not self-evident because they are in the Declaration of Independence; they are in that Document because they were self-evident to those who knew God. And because they knew God they sought for ways to please Him, and ways to form a permanent government, and ways to preserve the God-given Rights and the Independence they saw as a gift from God Himself.

However, over the past two hundred years we have moved from a Biblical society to a nation with a secular humanistic worldview. How is it that we see the Declaration of Independence differently than do those who signed that Document? Consider three reasons:

First is the matter of **Time**! Our memory remembers only that which is important to our immediate needs. Over time our school teachers – those who should know – either forgot or were not taught the truly vital information we should have learned in school.

A second reason why we view the Declaration of Independence different than did the signers is **Charles Beard** [1874-1948]! Beard was no doubt the most influential historian of the early 20th Century. He wrote a massive number of articles and text books that interpreted history for colleges and high schools. **His writings were designed to destroy the reputations of the Founding Fathers.** He painted them as selfish landowners and businessmen who framed the Declaration in such a way as to protect their own economic interests. At the same time Beard made the socialistic teachings of Karl Marx popular. So, instead of seeing the Founders as Christians they were portrayed by Professor Beard as men driven by self-interests. Beard, being a liberal, caused millions of Americans to embrace socialism. It is doubtful if the American people would have accepted President Franklin D. Roosevelt's New Deal had our culture not been prepared by Charles Beard. The intense conflict between labor and management that developed after World War I – and still exists today – is based on

Capital, a book by Karl Marx – and the teachings of Beard.

A third reason why we do not see the Declaration of Independence as they did in early America was because **we have not experienced a Great Awakening** as they did. Their Awakening prepared the Colonies for a cutting off of European selfishness and the creation of a distinctive Christian culture in its place. Had there been no spiritual Awakening there would have been no Declaration of Independence, no U.S. Constitution, no Bill of Rights, and no United States of America! But things have changed since the signing of that Declaration when the Founders pledged their Lives, their Fortunes and their Sacred Honor. We pledge virtually nothing – but expect everything in return. Can these bones live? We need the breath of God to grant us a personal and national Awakening!

In a very troubling sense our Founding Documents are no longer a perfect fit in our socialistic mindset. This does not mean the Documents should be scrapped – but that secular humanism should be scrapped. Jesus Christ is the sole author of Independence – and the Independence we want as a nation can only be had in Him! For in Him alone is protection and peace!

Schools, if they followed the Founders' intent, would be teaching the relationship between the Bible and the Declaration of Independence, and the part both played in the Founding of America. The Bible, if truth be told, would be recognized and endorsed for what it is: The Master Founding Document of America! If we do not return to our original foundation, Martin Luther's prophecy will most certainly come true, that **"schools will prove to be great gates of hell unless they diligently labor in explaining the Holy Scriptures, engraving them in the hearts of youth."**[108] The Foundation of America – as embodied in the Founding Document, the Declaration of Independence – is being eroded. King David still asks a question we must answer: *"If the foundations be destroyed, what can the righteous do?"* [Psalm 11:3]

The most remembered feature of the Declaration of Independence is its reference to the three Inalienable Rights: Life, Liberty and the pursuit of Happiness. The most forgotten but vital feature of the Declaration is the last paragraph where we declared ourselves *absolved from all Allegiance to the British Crown, and that all political connection with Great Britain is totally dissolved.*

Some people came to America for business purposes. But the prime movers were Christians who required Liberty of conscience to fulfill their God-ordained purpose. Independence meant different things to these two peoples. The Christians could not freely obey God if their lives were under an oppressive regime. This is amply experienced by Christians who longed for freedom in the old Soviet Union – and in present-day China, Cuba, Iran, North Korea and many more lands.

Old England oppressed the human spirit. She had become spiritually bankrupt. The German Reformation that took place 250 years earlier was practically forgotten. Great Britain, once influenced by Wyclif, Knox, Bunyan, Calvin and Luther, had not totally forgotten God. They simply repackaged Him into a religious system controlled by men. Similar to the Church of Rome that claimed to be the only reservoir of eternal grace and the keepers of the gates to heaven, the Church of England allowed no Liberty of conscience or worship without her permission. Britain had an oppressive tax system designed to enrich England at the expense of the American Colonies. The British Church was destitute; the British Crown was oppressive.

The Great Awakening cut off the American Culture from European influence, and the Declaration of Independence finalized the deal, making it legal and guaranteeing God-given Rights to every citizen.

God approved! Providence put the final authorization on the transaction by transplanting the spiritual life of the Great Awakening into the Colonial culture by means of the Declaration of Independence. Their **firm reliance on the protection of divine Providence** was sweetly rewarded with victory against overwhelming odds.

The Great Awakening delivered the inner man from sin. The Declaration of Independence declared the outer man free from British controls. The War for Independence that followed secured every square inch of land, every business, every person, every tax, every home, out from under the hand of Britain, and placed them into the hands of Americans who would soon choose a Government to their liking, one that would protect those Rights that Britain had so desperately tried to steal.

Something has happened to our independence, the independence as understood by our Founders. Because independence is vitally linked with a spiritual Awakening – as it was with our Founders – we cannot have one without the other: Spiritual independence comes with spiritual Awakening. Where the Awakening is absent, independence will lead us away from God; where men are spiritually awake and alert, independence will be seen for what it is: a Gift from God!

In Colonial History, the answer to the question – Can These Bones Live? – was a resounding **"Yes!"** Today, another Declaration of Independence is needed – or a resurrection of the old one! Can we find fifty-six men who have the "sacred honor" to willingly pledge their lives and their fortunes to so vital a cause? Independence – rightly understood – is still worth fighting for!

15 – RIGHTS AND FREEDOMS DEFINED

We Americans understand little about the Declaration of Independence and even less about Freedoms and Rights. They are often considered to be one and the same. We usually grab for the one we think will work best for us when someone gets in the way of our progress.

So we ask – Is there a difference between a Right and a Freedom? If so, what is it? In 2008 a group of churchmen got together to compose **An Evangelical Manifesto**. The group included several church leaders, among them Os Guinness and Dallas Willard [an emerging church leader, a movement we will consider later]. The lengthy Manifesto dealt with many issues, but we limit our consideration regarding their use of the word **Rights**: The **Manifesto** says **"every right we assert for ourselves is at once a right we defend for others. A right for a Christian is a right for a Jew, and a right for a secularist, and a right for a Mormon, and right for a Muslim, and a right for a Scientologist, and right for all the believers in all the faiths across this wide land."**[109] This is current thinking but it is not Biblical! A father or mother has the freedom and power to abuse a child, but no Right to do so. Freedom has to do with ability and opportunity; a Right has to do with a God-given Moral Choice.

God's First Commandment reads: *Thou shalt have no other gods before Me!* [Ex.20:3] That Commandment was not only binding on Israel, but also on all persons and nations because God owns the world and made it for His glory. We have the Freedom to disobey that Commandment but at our own peril. We have Freedom to disobey, but not the Right to do so. We may exercise the Freedom to be a Scientologist, a Muslim, or an Atheist, but we have no such Biblical Right. We have a Right to worship the true God. We have the Right to follow Jesus Christ, but we have no Right to follow demons or heretics. As a Christian-based country, we open our doors to all religions – and that is the thing to do. That does not mean that every other religion has the same Biblical Right as Christianity. That being the case, neither does the Christian have the Right to deny other religions the Freedom to exist and go the direction they prefer.

For our Founders, Freedom **from** sin was not Freedom **to** sin. As the Spirit of God swept across America's landscape during the Great Awakening it became very clear that no one had a Right to sin, and those who exercised that Freedom were frowned upon. Wherever sin was found in Colonial America, whether it was pride, hypocrisy or sins of the flesh, the perpetrators were pressed to repent. In the eternal judgment of God, none will boldly declare: **"God, You gave me the Right to be a pagan!"** Or, **"God, You gave me a Right to sin!"** No, you have the freedom to sin, but there is no such right!

Is self-defense a Right? In his book **Constitutional Law**, John Randolph Tucker [1823-1897], Attorney-General for the State of Virginia over a hundred years ago, wrote, ". . . **Self-preservation, embracing** self-defense and self-development to the highest degree possible, is a religious duty. Man not only may, but must, defend himself. Self-defense is not merely a Right; it is a duty – a religious duty."[110] Tucker fully embraced the 2nd Amendment on the Right to keep and bear arms!

What about suicide? Is it a Right? May I do with my body what I please? The Law of Nature, installed by God when He created Man, requires that life be preserved. Because life is God-created and precious, neither abortion nor suicide is a Right. A wrong can never be a right! Dietrich Bonhoeffer tells us, **"Even if his earthly life has become a torment for him, he must commit it intact into God's hand, from which it came, and he must not try to break free by his own efforts, for in dying he falls again into the hand of God, which he found too severe while he lived."[111]**

There is a growing softness in America: Tucker's contention that self-defense is a Right and a religious duty is considered to be from another era. We no longer want to fight as a nation even when our enemy is distinctly evil. **Instead of fighting evil we have embraced the idea that fighting is evil!** Although this thinking was around during Colonial days, it was overcome by staunch and steadfast Christians who had put the nation's interests ahead of their own. As the British continued to deprive the American Colonies of more Rights and constantly interfered with their Freedoms, more and more people – primarily Christians – spoke up. Patrick Henry, an outspoken Christian lawyer from Virginia, was one of these. On March 23, 1775, at St. John's Church in Richmond, Virginia, before the Virginia Convention, Henry began his speech by saying, **"For my own part I consider it as nothing less than a question of freedom or slavery."** And concluded with these famous words: **"Is life so dear, or peace so sweet, as to be purchased at the price of chains and slavery? Forbid it, Almighty God! I know not what course others may take; but as for me, give me liberty or give me death!"**[112]

Another leader of righteousness – though the British called him a rebel – was Peter Muhlenberg, the Lutheran preacher in Virginia. After a Sunday morning service, Pastor Muhlenberg took off his clerical robe, revealing the uniform of an officer in George Washington's Army. Proceeding to the church steps, he enlisted 300 men who joined him as he marched off to aid General Washington in the battle for Liberty.

When the cause is just, it is just to fight! However, there is a religious philosophy today that says man is basically good, sin is an outdated topic: God is for peace, and the time of war is over. This has taken the fight out of the hearts of many an American – and confused many a Christian. When the War for Independence began, many liberal preachers quickly sailed back to England. Most of these, of course, were Church of England preachers loyal to the Crown. On the other hand, Bible-believers stayed and fought, such as Patrick Henry, Peter Muhlenberg and a host of others whom God was willing to bless with His Hand of Providence. The conservative fights not merely to defend himself: He also fights to defend the Rights of his fellowman.

The defense of one's life would be optional if that life was not a gift from God. However, because our life is not our own – but belongs to Him who created it – our obligation is not to our own comfort but to Him. *You are not your own, for you have been bought with a price...* [1 Cor.6:20; 7:23]

If Rights come from Government, then Government is the final authority – to be respected and unquestioningly obeyed. If Rights come from God then he is the final authority who deserved ultimate obedience. This should be a serious concern for every citizen as Government increases in power. It is already against the law in several countries to read certain portions of Scripture from the pulpit regarding God's judgment against certain lifestyles. It is against the law in China to have more than one child per couple; the second child must be aborted. Here is the case where the Chinese government has over-ruled God. With the growth of Christianity in China [Christians now number up to 130 million], that nation will either yield to the laws of God or collapse in its fight against His people.

Non-believers say, *"Our lips are our own: Who is Lord over us?"* [Psalm 12:4] The Apostle Peter was not of this persuasion: He spoke the Truth for his lips were not his own. When he was told by the authorities not to preach Jesus and the Resurrection, he said: *"We cannot but speak the things that we have seen and heard!"* [Acts 4:18-20] Peter was not confrontational: He was simply doing what God

161

asked of him. Nevertheless, he was thrown into prison; then an angel let him out and told him: *"Go, stand and speak all the words of this Life."* [Acts 5:20] In order for Peter to obey the angel's orders, he had to disobey religious leaders!

"Thou shalt have no other gods before Me," is God's First Commandment [Exodus 20:3; Deuteronomy 5:7]. Not only the first in order but the first in importance – for all others hinge on that one Commandment. Jesus Christ came into the world to die on the Cross, removing our self-worship and self-management. Jesus Christ brings us to the place of **having no gods before God!**

One of the many amazing things about God is that He grants us the Freedom to be rebellious, obnoxious, bitter, self-pitying, angry and resentful toward Him and His world and toward our own circumstances – even though we do not have a Biblical Right to retain any of these attitudes. Another amazing thing is that, through the cleansing Blood of Jesus Christ, God rejoicingly welcomes us back into fellowship with Him. It is difficult for the person whose life has fallen into disorder and confusion to trust God – and yet, that is the very one God stoops down to touch in Jesus Christ. The defeated, the humiliated and the exploited are especially near to the mercy of God. It is to the undisciplined that Jesus Christ offers His help and strength. Those who have gone astray can still hear the call of Jesus Christ: *"Come unto me . . . and I will give you rest – for My yoke is easy and My burden is light!"* [Matthew 11:28-30]

Our Freedoms get us into trouble [it all started with Adam's Freedom], but Oh how precious is the cleansing and help we find in Jesus Christ. It is understandable why angels rejoice in heaven when a sinner returns.

When Jesus saves us He removes Wrongs from the heart and empowers us to do Right. Peter wrote, *"He Himself bore our sins in His body on the cross, that we might die to sin and live to righteousness; for by His wounds you were healed. In the past you continually strayed like sheep, but now you have returned to the Shepherd and Guardian of your souls."* [1 Pet.2:24-25] The Christian has Freedom to sin but refuses to do so, choosing rather to please the One who saved him!

16 – ETHICS LOST

Ethics is more than a field of study for a college student: It is a set of principles to live by. There are two kinds of Ethics: One is based on the Knowledge of Good and Evil that came from the serpent in the Garden of Eden; the other is based on the Knowledge of God in the one who is made right with God through the death of Jesus Christ and the working of the Spirit of God in his life. The non-Christian, when concerned with Ethics, asks: **"How can I be good?"** For his answer he looks to himself and his own knowledge of good and evil, gathering all the facts he can, assuming he has the wisdom to know and the strength to do what he decides is the right ethical route to take. He then gives himself the self-congratulations he feels he deserves for making a man-wise decision, which he has no way of knowing whether it is right or pleasing to God.

Christian Ethics, on the other hand, asks: **"What is the Will of God?"** The Christian, refusing to trust his own wisdom, finds the answer to his quest in the Bible and in obedience to the Spirit of God.

Polonius is a character in Shakespeare's Hamlet, and is best known for giving the advice: **"To thine own self be true!"** Because of the spiritual climate created by the Great Awakening, Polonius' counsel was ignored in the Colonies: They were not concerned with being true to themselves, but true to Jesus Christ! However, the slogan fit well in France, and is again embraced by Secular Humanists today in whatever land they promote their creed.

Ethics in Early America beckoned a man to be faithful to God and man. Today there is little study of Ethics in public schools because the foundation for ethical study has been removed from the school system. We would have to ask: If the Bible is not the basis for a solid Ethical study, what is? Every Colonist knew the Bible to be a solid foundation for an ethical life! Noah Webster said Ethics **"teaches men their duty and the reason for it,"** Modern dictionaries change that, telling us that ethic is **"The standard of character set up by any race or nation."**[113] The **"standard of character"** adopted by Jonathan Edwards as he studied the Bible was altogether different from the **"standard of character"** held by John Dewey who denied the existence of God. Edwards accepted the Bible as foundational in his understanding of his duties; Dewey said man needs no God; he will save himself. Dietrich Bonhoeffer advises in the opening paragraph in his book *Ethics* that **the first task of Christian ethics is to invalidate the knowledge of good and evil.**[114] The weakness of Dewey is that he has only his own knowledge of good and evil from which to draw information; the strength of Edwards comes from Jesus Christ, the One who lived a pure and perfect life.

In Colonial America, virtue meant manliness, and manliness meant independence. In that day the independent man relied on no other human for his care or keep. In fact, the only one who could vote in some states was the man who owned property. Property, of course, meant either land, or gold or silver coins in the pocket. Manliness also meant being in a position to take up arms and defend yourself as well as assist your neighbor in his defense. This might sound like a villainous society with daily gunfights. We have become accustomed to ease, making it probable that we would rather sleep than fight. **Instead of fighting evil we have come to believe fighting is evil!** Not so in Colonial America! Although the Colonists were independent men, they had just come through the Great Awakening; it was that spiritual Awakening that brought their Ethics in line with the Bible: They had come to believe that Rights were a precious gift from God, and that it was their responsibility to defend their neighbor's Rights as vigorously as they defended their own. This brought them into a unity that was similar to the unity men experience on the battle field as they face a common foe.

The Great Awakening brought thousands into a right relationship with God. Those new converts were not disconnected and isolated souls. They began to be knit together, not just in churches but in civil communities that cared for one another. Living as they were in the shadow and shelter of the Great Awakening, the very structure and composition of society had changed. Through the years there have been several Revivals or Awakenings: Each of them changed the hearts of individuals; some had an effect on the moral climate of society; but none changed the culture like the Great Awakening of the 1740s. God Himself impressed His own image on the land, both on the Church and on the culture. The Government, the Family, the Church – all were changed. The moral and ethical atmosphere was altered by the Hand of

Providence. No one had to teach his brother the rules of civility; these men intuitively knew, for Jesus Christ had affected both their private and public lives, bringing them in line with Biblical holiness. Like the apple tree that needs no instructor to tell it what kind of fruit to bear, these men needed no coach. **Intuitive righteousness exceeds artificial piety!**

The genuine Christianity of the Colonial Founders served as the basis for the Declaration of Independence, the Constitution and the ten original articles in the Bill of Rights. Roger Sherman was a signer of both Documents and was greatly appreciated by his colleagues for his wisdom and grace. Thomas Jefferson said of Sherman that he was **a man who has never said a foolish thing in his life.** And John Adams called Sherman . . . **an old Puritan, as honest as an angel and as firm in the cause of American Independence as Mount Atlas.**[115] Roger Sherman was spiritually alive because of the Great Awakening that occurred thirty-five years earlier. Sherman became a member of a Congregational Church pastored by Rev. Jonathan Edwards, the son of the great evangelist Jonathan Edwards whom God used in the Great Awakening. In one of his speeches, Sherman advised living **"no more to ourselves, but to him who loved us and gave himself to die for us."**[116] That is Ethics at its best!

Biblical Ethics is spontaneous – doing what is right! Only the Christian has this innate quality because his life is indwelt by the life of God. He needs no assistance from laws and rules. Paul knew this in his life, telling Timothy, **"we know that the**

law is not made for a righteous man." [1 Tim.1:9]
The righteous man does righteously! An apple tree
needs no one to tell it the size of the apple to be
grown. [Matthew 7:16] The man who walks by the
Spirit needs no assistance for **the righteousness of
the law is fulfilled in those who walk in the Spirit.**
[Rom.8:1-4]

For animals, the Law of Nature is found in their
instincts. For man, God's Law is found in the Ten
Commandments, which requires our cooperation.
Government is installed to enforce this Law of Nature,
punishing those who do evil and rewarding those
who do well. According to Dietrich Bonhoeffer, **"for
this purpose the government is given the sword.**
Bonhoeffer concludes that **whenever the sword of
government is no longer willing to serve the law of
God . . . they must be made subject to the law of
God by the proclamation of the Church.** In addition,
Bonhoeffer tells us that **"It was sin that made
necessary the divine institution of government.
The sword which God has given to government
is to be used by it in order to protect men against
the chaos which is caused by sin. Government is
to punish the criminal and to safeguard life.**[117]

The Church does not use the sword to produce
ethical behavior – although it has done this in the
past. Rather, it proclaims the Truth of Jesus Christ.

Three basic essentials existed in Colonial
America: **Providence, Ethics** and **Liberty**. This
three-fold combination produced a Christian nation.
Without any one of the three elements there would

not have been a godly beginning – and without all three we shall not long continue!

Providence – God Himself – brought about the Great Awakening: That Awakening was not the work of effective orators like Edwards or Whitefield. These men and others were tools in the Divine Hand. God produced what He wanted in American culture.

Ethics and their true value are seen in the lives of the Founders. William Penn wrote: **"True Godliness doesn't turn men out of the World, but enables them to live better in it, and excites their endeavors to mend it."**[118] George Washington saw a connection between morals and the health of America, saying **"your practice of the moral and religious obligations, are the strongest claims to national and individual happiness."** Adding that **"a good moral character is the first essential in a man . . . It is therefore highly important that you should endeavor not only to be learned but virtuous."**[119] This is Ethics lived!

Liberty is the realm in which God Himself lives! This is the same Liberty He has graciously imparted to His own. To understand this Liberty think about Nebuchadnezzar, the King of Babylon: Having been driven to insanity, he ate grass with the animals for years because of his pride. When his sanity returned, he said, **the most High rules in the kingdom of men and gives it to whomsoever He chooses. And all the inhabitants of the earth are as nothing: and He does according to His own will in the army of heaven, and among the inhabitants of the earth: and none can stay His hand or say to Him,**

'What are you doing?' [Daniel 4:32-35] This is the Liberty in which God dwells and into which He takes believers, guiding them in His ways and toward His determined purposes. This is the Liberty addressed and secured by our Declaration of Independence. It is NOT the Liberty to please self, but a Liberty described by the Apostle Paul in Galatians 5:13: *"For, brethren, you have been called unto Liberty; only use not Liberty for an opportunity to serve the flesh, but by love serve one another."* If a man has no Liberty to please God, he has no Liberty at all!

The design of God – and our Founders – was that American society should be ethical and function smoothly. That could only happen if the Law of Nature was obeyed. It was never intended that the Liberty of one segment of society would or could deprive another sector of their Liberty. No Supreme Court decision was as obvious on this issue as the legalization of abortion; it had a tragic effect on the unborn as well as on the American culture as a whole. Life quickly became trivial and surplus matter. Life, once viewed as precious, no longer had value. William Blackstone evaluation on this topic is precious: He wrote, **"Life is the immediate gift of God, a right inherent by nature in every individual; and it begins in contemplation of law as soon as an infant is able to stir in the mother's womb. An infant in the mother's womb is capable of having a legacy, or a copyhold estate made to it. It may have a guardian assigned to it; and it is enabled to have an estate limited to its use . . . as if it were actually born."**[120] Our lawyers and judges no longer read Blackstone or the Bible, having been educated in humanistic institutions. So the value of life – the gift of God – continues to diminish.

As already shown, the Great Awakening had a liberating effect on the lives of individuals, families, culture, and the Government. That Awakening created a Christian Culture. On the opposite side however, the legalizing of abortion had a detrimental effect. Life, rather than being held as a gift from God, was now cheap. Not only are millions of babies being sacrificed on the altar of egocentric self, that fateful Court ruling resulted in school shootings, rapes and other self-gratifying crimes. Abortion, unthinkable in the minds of a husband and his wife on the wild prairie in Colonial days, is now blessed by the Court. That was not the **Liberty** in which God dwells – nor the Liberty secured by the Declaration of Independence.

We are no longer the nation founded by the Colonists. Ethics have changed; the culture has changed. A man may say he is ethical, but if his ethics are built firmly on the sandy beach, they will be eroded more and more by every wave of personal lust or longing. Self-centered interests are now protected by government. The Biblical ethicist is protected by Providence! How precious it was to welcome a new-born baby into the Colonial world; that is no longer true in millions of homes today. A mother's womb is the most dangerous place in America for a child. And the second most dangerous place is the public school which tells them they are the descendants of animals or slime.

There is a central issue that is often forgotten when dealing with abortion, euthanasia, murder, suicide or any other life-destructive measures. The body of any individual is the gift of God: There is no other means granted by God whereby the individual can function in this world except in his body. Jesus Himself said: *"A body You have prepared for Me . . . to do Thy will, O God!"* [Hebrews 10:5-7] When a body, any person's body, is deprived of life, there is no longer any possibility of doing the will of God on earth. Who is there among us that could arrogantly think himself wiser than God: He, having brought a life into this world is deprived of due worship by our arrogant act.

Once a person begins to violate either the Law of Nature or Revealed Law, the conscience begins to adjust itself to accommodate the violation. Example: When a young lad gets deeply angry the first time, he feels guilt. The second time he partially approves. The third and succeeding times he justifies his anger. After this the conscience sanctions, and the emotions endorse, the anger. This seems to be the same process, regardless of age, whether in the realm of lying, prostitution, stealing, adultery, pornography, cheating, etc. Conversion, deliverance, a Great Spiritual Awakening is needed wherein the Intense Presence of God re-shapes the inner core of the man. God then begins the process of **conforming the believer to the image of His Son** [Romans 8:29; 12:1-2], bringing his life in line with Biblical Ethics, pleasing to God and a blessing to man. The man who has experienced the breath of God can never be the same as he was in his pre-Christian existence!

172

17 – DIVERGENT RELIGION

Christianity differs today from what it was in Colonial times. It differs from Reformation days and from New Testament times. None of the prior times carried in it the "Positive" religion so prevalent today. Today's mantra is a New Age tune: "Don't tell me what you're against, but only what you're for!" This posture keeps the Church from having discernment.

Current Modernists explain Christianity by using the word Positive, implying that the Church of the past – in Paul's day, in Luther's day, in Colonial days – was too Negative; that we have found something Positive they knew nothing about.

The use of the word Positive might imply that present-day Christianity is not only inadequate but harmful and depressing. The word Positive is used to belittle the fundamentalist and is used to describe a Christianity that is inclusive, that embraces all peoples, whether evangelical or liberal. Positive Christianity might even include – with a little stretching here or there – the Moslem, the Mormon, Eastern religion or any other cult or sect. The word Positive carries with it little or no restrictions – especially as it falls from the mouth of Robert Schuller. The door is wide open! The insinuation is that Jesus would approve such a gracious attitude.

Or would He? Schuller is not the first to come up with the concept of Positive Christianity. It was a term used in Hitler's Germany and adopted by Nazi leaders to make Christianity compatible with National Socialism. Hitler's brand, to be sure, was quite different than Schuller's: Traditional Christianity has always emphasized orthodoxy, but Hitler labeled his brand as *"Positive Christianity"* to distinguish it from orthodoxy. Hitler's Positivism saw Jesus hating the Jews. Genuine Christianity reveals Jesus dying for Jew and Gentile alike. Nazis professed to love the historical Jesus but not the orthodox Jesus. In that way they could pick out the sayings of Jesus that fit their political purpose. Schuller's brand of "Positive Christianity" is quite difference: While Hitler used Jesus for political advantage, Schuller uses Jesus to emphasize optimistic improvement. In either case the word is adjusted and the simple meaning of the stand-alone, all-powerful word – **Christianity** – is lost.

The Bible offers Realism: That is, it deals with things as they are. Perhaps it was Schuller who started the modern use of Positive Christianity, but he is not alone in depleting the life out of Real Christianity. He does remain a major player in the transition, changing Biblical terms into something other than those defined in the Bible. Schuller defines Hell as the **Loss of pride**; Born Again as having a **Positive self-image**; and Christ as **Self-Esteem Incarnate**.

Schuller has an advantage over previous promoters of Positive Christianity: He has newer Bible versions upon which to draw: They lend themselves to looseness in the translating process, so that the reader often fails to touch reality but touches instead a "feel-good" religion.

In 863 B.C., Ahab was the King of Israel; Jehoshaphat ruled Judah. In 1 Kings 22 we find a story about a day when King Jehoshaphat visited King Ahab. Ahab had Biblical reasons to believe that the city of Ramoth-Gilead belonged to him [Deut.4:43]. So he wanted Jehoshaphat's help in getting it back from Syria. To get solid counsel on the matter Ahab brought together 400 of his "feel-good" prophets. These prophets of Baal were unanimous: **Invade Syria!** They said. Jehoshaphat still had doubts, so they called one more prophet named Micaiah, a prophet of God, who said: *"I see all Israel scattered upon the hills. . ."* As Ahab went off to battle he said: *"Put Micaiah in prison until I return in peace."* So, as Micaiah went off to prison he said: *"If you return in peace, the Lord has not spoken by me!"* [v.28] Micaiah the realist was right, for Ahab did not return: He was killed in battle. So much for Positivism!

Positive Christianity rejects nothing and no one – except the fundamentalist. Even Muslims and Eastern religions are sought out for counsel, but the strict Biblicist is shunned. The reason is simple enough: The Bible-believer knows Biblical truth is absolute. He believes the Bible when it says that Jesus Christ is the only way to the Father [John 14:6; Acts 4:12] The Positivist moves outside of Bible truth and sees many ways to God. After all, he asks out loud, who really knows what truth is? Due to his sweet smile and noticeable gentleness, few perceive his error or resist his heresy. Those who do oppose his Positive Christianity are charged with being judgmental.

The following is a recent example of Positive Christianity. Following are selections from an article in the Wall Street Journal by WSJ reporter Michael

Phillips on December 19th, 2005. It can be found on the LighthouseTrails website, and is given here simply as a realistic warning. The article tells us that Bruce Wilkinson, the author of the popular book, **Prayer of Jabez**, **"resigned in a huff from the African charity he founded."** Wilkinson had moved to Africa with his family in 2002 with the hopes of rescuing one million orphans.

The article states: **"Mr. Wilkinson won churchloads of followers in Swaziland but left them bereft and confused . . . his departure left critics convinced he was just another in a long parade of outsiders who have come to Africa making big promises and quit the continent when local people didn't bend to their will."**

In October of 2003, Bruce Wilkinson spoke at Robert Schuller's Crystal Cathedral and said, **"I want to talk about dreams. Of all places in the world to talk about dreams this is the place ... because I think Dr. Schuller is the patriarch in the work about living your dream."** Wilkinson's book, **_The Dream Giver_**, had come out just one month earlier and he gave his message at the Crystal Cathedral based on the book. One week later, Wilkinson spoke at Rick Warren's Saddleback Church and shared a similar message.

Bruce Wilkinson's message about **_"God's Dream"_** led to the formation of **_Dream for Africa_**, an organization founded by Wilkinson. Wilkinson had planned to build a large orphanage in Swaziland, Africa, one which according to the Wall Street Journal article would have a bed-and-breakfast, game reserve, bible college, industrial park and Disneyesque tourist destination. Wilkinson who has taught that believers can receive blessings from God by reciting Jabez's 33 word prayer had felt confident that his dream for Africa would become a reality.

The Wall Street Journal said that **"Rick Warren, who considers Wilkinson a very close friend, told his congregation in 2003 that Wilkinson's dream should be their dream too."**[121] Positive Christianity sounds good from the pulpit but fails in the crisis hour because it relies on human wisdom and human ability, not on Jesus Christ. Paul tells us it is only in Christ the promises of God are Positive [2 Cor.1:20]. All that is outside of Jesus Christ will sooner or later come to naught!

The Colonial Church may not have been what today is defines as *"spiritually alive"* because it was not *"exciting,"* but the preacher was loyal to Christian Scriptures and could be trusted. He was generally a man with a pure heart. His ministry did not rest on the salary he received. Church of England preachers were accustomed to receiving a salary from state funds. Colonial pastors often supported themselves by various means, as teachers, lawyers, farmers or business owners. While Scripture tells us the laborer is worthy of pay, especially those who labor in the Word, this was not used by the preacher to pressure the congregation for higher wages. Money was not an issue for a Colonial pastor. The man of God was generally poor – but free from the greed so prevalent in the Church today: This greed is usually disguised as entrepreneurial wisdom.

Pastors, at a Conference in the mid-1900s, were encouraged to tell their church boards that pastors should receive a salary equal to that of the average layman's salary in the Church, perhaps even more. After all, the pastor is worth more than the average man because of the eternal message he brings. How many of the pastors fell for this sly approach I do not know. When a pastor gets his eyes on the size of his salary or the dimensions of his home he forgets that he is a man whose purpose is to be a living demonstration of Jesus Christ, who had nowhere to lay His head.

Colonial Christians were reserved; today there is a looseness and at times emotional excess. In Colonial days there was a deep reverence in the meeting place because of their profound respect for God and the Bible. Today God is portrayed as light-hearted. Because He loves everybody immensely, sin is not taken too seriously – and in the process, God and grace are not taken very seriously either. God is seen as appreciating the half-hearted more than the rigid absolutist who might offend people with his orthodox views.

A deep reverence – even for the church building – existed in Colonial days. This continued on even into the 1950s when no one walked into the sanctuary while the pastor was praying or while a vocalist was singing a special number. Once a person was in the sanctuary there was only slight whispering and very little walking around, even if one arrived early: This created an atmosphere that told visitors we are here to meet with God. That seemed to change with the introduction of the Charismatic Movement. Our deductions here are not meant as a blanket criticism of the movement, but there are elements that need addressing. While the Pentecostals [forerunners to the Charismatics] said one had to tarry for the Holy Spirit – days, months or years if necessary – the Charismatics said we can receive the Spirit without waiting another moment. Soon, this **immediacy principle** was employed for a host of other spiritual blessings one might want, from salvation to healing to finances. The Charismatic Movement created a smorgasbord of blessing, with everything already paid for! It cost nothing; it was free! Come and get it! Soon the whole evangelical Church joined the Charismatics in the spiritual diner. Robert Schuler, Rick Warren, Bill Hybels and a host of others, whether Charismatics or not, would have no ministry today if the Charismatic Movement had not opened wide the door.

In Colonial America, the church, the school and the home saw to it that children became **"wise and virtuous."** That was the goal of education. Today it seems more important that children feel good about themselves even if they are neither wise nor virtuous; even if they are failures in school. As a result, the most worthless among us are as happy as the productive! This was not tolerated in Colonial society.

Some might contend that Colonial Christianity was not "modernized" so as to understand what we understand today. The Colonial pastor taught that the man who confesses his sin finds that Jesus is indeed a Friend of sinners – but not a friend of the proud.

God still resists the proud but gives grace to the humble [James 4:6]. We moderns might not think the Founders were as genuine as we are but, with the general carnality and the heresy that has invaded the present-day Church, our Founders might very well be justified in thinking **WE** are not true believers!

It was most important in the Colonial Church to be a responsible member of the community. It is most important in today's Church to have fun and be entertained.

Who, we ask, is a true Christian? Noah Webster defines it for us in his 1828 Dictionary of the English Language, saying that a Christian is **"A real disciple of Christ; one who believes in the truth of the Christian religion, and studies to follow the example, and obey the precepts, of Christ; a believer in Christ who is characterized by real piety."** Such a one fulfills Webster's definition in any age!

Timothy Dwight, the grandson of Jonathan Edwards, was president of Yale College from 1795 till his death in 1817. When he arrived at Yale there were few Christians at the school – perhaps five or six. Dwight, a zealous believer, became deeply burdened for his students, often addressing them regarding the **"infidel philosophy"** in America: Today that philosophy is known as secular humanism. When he finished his presidency at Yale it was nearly impossible to find a non-Christian in the student body. It was not that Dwight kept them out; he accepted them and brought them to faith in Christ with his clear presentation of truth in Jesus Christ. He knew their eternal destiny hinged on their relationship with Jesus Christ, and so did the future destiny of America. Dwight said: **"Without religion we may possibly retain the freedom of savages, bears, and wolves, but not the freedom of New England. If our religion were gone, our state of society would perish with it, and nothing would be left."** [122] Perhaps Dwight was speaking to our generation as much as to his own student body, for we are getting dangerously close to forsaking Christianity. No, we are not neglecting religion altogether: We are simply substituting a pick-your-own religion. Any god will do! This transfer away from genuine Christianity to the false is speeded up as liberal media and college professors mock and ridicule the genuine out of the public square and out of the classroom.

Samuel Chase [1741-1811] was appointed to the U.S. Supreme Court by George Washington. In the case of Runkel v. Winemiller, 1799, Justice Case gave the Court's opinion in which he wrote: **"By our form of government, the Christian religion is the established religion,. . ."** [123] and as late as 1931 the U.S. Supreme Court agreed, saying in United States v. Macintosh: **"We are a Christian people. . ."** [124] Jesus Christ is God's Son: By His act of creation, His Incarnation, Crucifixion and Resurrection, He became the rightful heir and owner of the world [Psalm 2:6-12; Colossians 1:16-17; Revelation 4:11]. Our American Founders understood this to be of God's choosing, and therefore honored any and all Protestant denominations, but not the non-Christian religions. **America was a Christian Nation!** This was fitting, not only in the Founders' views, but in God's as well; for He has set His King – Jesus – upon the Throne to rule the earth and heaven. Our Founders could trace America's very existence back to the Providential Hand of God in the Great Awakening, in the breaking away from the decayed culture of Europe, and in the establishing of the United States as a free and independent nation. They understood that Jesus Christ brought America into existence. The Founders did not see themselves as having an option: Jesus Christ was the King to be honored.

Christianity has come to mean any one of many things. There was a time in early America when the term Christian meant a loyal follower of Jesus Christ; one who had been born again; had the assurance of salvation; and lived a virtuous life. He was usually referred to as a Conservative, one who believed in the fundamentals of the faith. Narrowing our definition down to simplicity we agree with Webster that Christianity is, **"the system of doctrines and precepts taught by Christ, and recorded by the evangelists and apostles."** To avoid doctrine is to avoid Jesus Christ.

There is nothing more important to the ambitious pastor than progress. If there is no progress it is important that he makes it look like there is! When things become routine it is time for change: Introduce a new program, a new business plan, a new staff member, restructure the church board, urge the construction of a new wing on the church building, or create an innovative mission to stop AIDS in Africa. Anything that looks like progress!

All this is so much activity – but who are we to judge another man's servant. Before his own Lord he stands or falls. Dietrich Bonhoeffer says the fanatic runs ahead of God while the reluctant lags behind. It is important that the motive behind the activity flow from the will of God, and is NOT done with fleshly ambition. We in the Church are so good at matching the world step for step. What the world does, we do! Jesus set our example, saying: ***Whatever the Father does, I do!*** [John 5:19]

When a church gets to be a certain size, we hire a business manager. He is chosen for his organizational skills, not his life in Christ. Hopefully he will be a spiritual man too, but if not, organization is a singular must. The Organizational Man in each of us, the Purpose-Driven, the Dream-Driven, the I-Can-Do-It Man, wars against the gentle Spirit of Jesus. The spiritual man, regardless of his training, senses when a program is not of God. Many an otherwise good man falls prey to Church Growth attractions.

The will of God for the preacher is found in Jesus' instructions to Paul following his conversion: **"For I have appeared to thee for this purpose . . . To open their eyes, and to turn them from darkness to light, and from the power of Satan unto God, that they might receive forgiveness of sins. . ."** [Acts 26:15-18] Godly preachers, both in Colonial days and today, are those who have experienced the breath of God! They are not more wise, clever, artful or crafty: They have the life of God.

The Colonial Church was unlike the Organizational Church of today. They had no worship team, no youth pastor, no business manager, no grounds supervisor; yet, they had conversions, baptisms, spiritual growth, a Biblical message, and above all else, the life of God. The pastor had a practical message, which included more than the simple Gospel. The four to five hour service covered many topics, especially during the days when the Red Coats were seeking control of society on behalf of the Church of England and the British Crown. Not all things were spiritual – but none of us are in a position to judge them for what they lacked. Their goal was to declare the simple message of salvation and have a place where they were sure the Word was faithfully taught to their children so they would be wise and virtuous.

Today there are many distractions: In the material realm the pastor expects a nice home, health insurance, a comfortable retirement plan, an adequate salary, a two to three-week vacation and hopefully a sabbatical. In the spiritual realm the attractions are far more enticing: Whatever will make the Church grow seems legitimate. Whether in the material or spiritual world, every attraction detracts from the pastor's call and cause. There are only two categories: For Christ and against Him. There is no substitute for Jesus Christ; nor is He on a par with other attractions: He stands alone!

While a student at St. Paul Bible College [now Crown College] in the 1950s, students had the privilege of hearing many missionaries. I recall a Pastor Tiggart who ministered in Japan following World War II. He said when the invitation to receive Jesus Christ was given in Japan, everyone raised their hands. Missionaries had difficulty convincing the Japanese that, to receive Jesus Christ they must give up their other gods. They would gladly receive Jesus if they could add Him to their current collection. After all — they thought — 330 gods are better than 329!

Sadly, the Church today is turning again to the East for spiritual enlightenment. Recall, it was the Spirit of God that closed the door to the North and to the East, sending Paul West to Macedonia. From there the Gospel continued its Westerly trek until it reached America. Observe what the prophet Ezekiel has to say about the worship of the gods of the East.

In the sixth year, as I sat in my house, the hand of the Lord fell upon me and the glory of the God of Israel was there; and He said to me: Do you see these great abominations? And I saw idols of the house of Israel. Then He said: Do you see what the elders of Israel do in the dark, in the chambers of their imagination? For they say, The Lord does not see me, and He has forsaken the earth. Again the Lord said: Have you seen even greater abomination? Then He brought me into the inner court of the Lord's temple and there I saw twenty-five men who had turned their backs on the temple of the Lord and were worshipping toward the East. Oh, Ezekiel! Is it a light thing to the house of Judah that they commit these abominations and provoked me to anger? Therefore, I will deal in vicious wrath; I shall not have pity. Because they said, The Lord hath forsaken the earth, I will repay them. [From Ezek. 8:1-18; 9:9-10]

The Church is going against the warning of Ezekiel, looking to gods of the East. An increasing number of pastors feel that Hindus and Buddhists have a measure of light that just might be a help to us moderns. Under the Self-Help section of a Christian Book Club, in the **Follow Christ** section, the first book listed is ***Holy Yoga***. Yoga is based on Hinduism, and its main goal is "union" with Brahman, a Hindu god. The various Yoga positions have names – and they are the names of Hindu goddesses and were named as worship to those goddesses. To practice Yoga – whether under the name Christian or Hinduism – is spiritually dangerous because evil spirits are involved. Yoga cannot be converted to being Christian no more than can light dwell with darkness, or Christ with Satan. The argument that Buddha is another name for Christ, and Christ is another name for Buddha, is heresy. The angel said to Mary: *"Fear not, Mary: For thou hast found favor with God, and shall conceive in thy womb and bring forth a Son, and shall call His Name JESUS. He shall be great and shall be called the Son of the Highest."* [Luke 1:30-33] Jesus Christ is the Son of the Living God; the One born to a Virgin in a manger in Bethlehem; the One who did miracles for three years in Judaea and Galilee; the One who was crucified and rose again – He is the Son of God who owns the world; He is the true God, the only legitimate object of worship!

Eastern religion believes in pluralism; that is, there are many paths to God, many sages and many holy books. Eastern religion excludes Christianity from their *"many paths to God"* because Christians believe in one Holy Book – the Bible; and in one Holy Savior, the Lord Jesus Christ. The Bible gives the guidelines as to who is a Christian: It is one who accepts the Bible as God's Word to man; and it is one who receives Jesus Christ as the Father's designated Savior of the world. The Bible is clear: *In the beginning was the Word . . . and all things were made by Him; and without Him was not anything made that was made. And the Word was made flesh, and dwelt among us, and we beheld His glory, the glory as of the only Begotten of the Father, full of grace and truth.* [John 1:1-3, 14] *All things were created by Jesus Christ and for Him, and He is before all things, and by Him all things hold together.* [From Col.1:12-17]

Jesus Christ is central. He is the One referred to in the First of the Ten Commandments: *"Thou shalt have no other gods before Me!"* [Exodus 20:3] He is the One whom Isaiah refers to as *"the Mighty God."* [Isaiah 9:6] He is the One whom John calls *"the Almighty."* [Rev.1:8]

Shortly after I was converted I began attending a Bible-believing Church in Oconomowoc, Wisconsin. I was soon questioned by the pastor of my former church who explained the errors of this new church regarding the second coming of Jesus, communion, etc. He then asked: **"David, what do you have to say for yourself?"** I did not realize it, but I must have memorized Romans 8:38-39, for immediately, without premeditation, I said: *"I am persuaded that neither death nor life nor angels nor principalities, nor powers nor things present nor things to come,*

*nor height nor depth nor any other creature shall
be able to separate me from the love of God which is
in Christ Jesus our Lord."* I then asked: **"What else
do you want me to have?"** to which he said: **"That
is the faith you want!"** and walked out. Since those
early days of my Christian walk my burning desire
has been to see Jesus Christ honored in His Church,
with no competitor vying for His throne. One thing,
however, I did not realize: There are at least three
classes of "Christians!" The first class says: **"I'm
not interested in spiritual things, but if I am
going to get to heaven I better believe in Jesus!"** A
second group says: **"All the evidence points to the
truth that Jesus is who the Bible says He is – the
Savior who died and rose, so I have decided to
trust in Him!"** That is commendable! A third class
is composed of those who have been apprehended
by Jesus Christ [Phil.3:12], have the witness of the
Spirit that they are children of God [Romans 8:16]
and have the blessing of Providence in their lives.
[Romans 8:28].

The Church, the Bride of Christ, once had eyes
only for her Master. Today she shows affection for
others. She not only looks with favor to the East,
she is also inventing her own heresy – the Emerging
church. The Church, the true Bride of Christ, with
warmth and zeal, held to Him and the doctrines of
the faith, preaching the Old-Time Gospel message
of forgiveness and attempts to reach non-Christians
with the Gospel. But along came a few men who had
visions of uniting with Moslems, Mormons, Eastern
Religions and the Liberal denominations. Rather

than seeking conversions these pastors felt that these religious people would be more open to the Gospel if they were accepted just as they are. Thus, religious people of all persuasions were embraced as though they were already in the Kingdom – or at least well on the way. Evidence of conversion was not essential. After all, they said, no one really knows the heart of another! Soon Emergents embraced mysticism, rituals, prayer beads, labyrinths, yoga or other Romish, Anglican and Eastern religious practices. The Bride of Christ could not find her way home!

There are very few tenets in the emerging church. The ones that are there might look like this: [1] Thou shalt not believe Jesus Christ is the only Savior of the world! [2] Thou shalt not judge or evaluate another! [3] Thou shalt not refuse the spiritual counsel of anyone! [4] Thou shalt not reject ancient mysticism! [5] Thou shalt not be dogmatic about anything!

The Emerging church is not a denomination but a loosely knit group of folks who, disappointed with the current church scene, reach into the past to find roots. Their cynicism to blames the existing Church when, in the heart is an unwillingness to go through the narrow door and walk with others who have walked through that door. Sometimes the Emerging church harkens back to Abraham; sometimes to Mohammed; sometimes to the early Church Fathers; sometimes to Mary; all in hopes of finding a way to God that avoids Jesus, never going back to Him alone. Two days after the 9-11 attack on New York, a major leader in the emerging church went to a mosque to meet with Moslems and *"build bridges"* with them.

The Emergents are gentle toward everyone except Bible believers. This is due to the Bible believers' resistance to the all-inclusive message Emergents preach – as would be the Apostle Paul! Emergents open their heart and emotions to everyone – except those who preach redemption in Jesus Christ only.

The Colonial Church was fortunate **not** to have an assortment of deceptive attractions. They certainly fought the darkness of that day, but the battle lines were different: The Old-Time preacher in America urged listeners to seek God until they had the witness of the spirit that they were born again. He was neither patted on the back nor told how good he was. He was told early that his only goodness was through faith in Jesus Christ.

Today Emergents embrace many things: Evangelicals, Neo-evangelicals, Liberals, New-Agers, Modernists, Post-Moderns, those who are Christians but don't know it, those who are good people in non-Christian religions, well-intentioned Moslems, fully-devoted Mormons, Romans Catholics, Eastern Mystics and many, many more. The words of Jesus do not fit: **"Enter by the narrow gate, for the gate is wide and the way broad that leads to destruction; and many enter by it. For the gate is small and the way narrow that leads to life—and few find it!"** [Matthew 7:13-14]

The Church – without the Master's permission – has widened the narrow gate!

Many new books by many emerging authors are converting countless pastors and skeptics to a revolutionary worldview.[132C] That worldview is basic Gnosticism; the Gnostic believes man can have a mystical relationship with God while shunning God's Son and designated Savior – Jesus Christ! John, prompted by the Spirit of God, said: **"Whoever denies the Son denies the Father: the one who confesses the Son has the Father also."** [1 John 2:23]

You will understand if names are omitted from the following quotes. It would serve no benefit to include them. The purpose of this section is not to tell you which authors to avoid and which to read; but that you might be drawn to truth and repelled by heresy – and be able to discern the difference when you hear it. Following a man is dangerous to your spiritual health: Some church leaders who seemed pure enough in their doctrine and declarations a year ago are now leaning into the emerging church camp. One prominent emerging leader scoffs at the second coming of Jesus Christ as a **"skyhook,"** and calls hell **"false advertising for God,"** and criticizes the Cross. Another says there is **"divine potential in every human being,"** a teaching that comes out of Eastern religion. Still another, a most famous California preacher says: **"I met once more with the Grand Mufti (a Muslim), truly one of the great Christ-honoring leaders of faith. . ."** Adding: **"Standing before a crowd of devout Muslims with the Grand Mufti, I know that we're all doing God's work together. Standing on the edge of a new millennium, we're laboring hand in hand to repair the breach."** He fails to see that Sharia law is gradually taking over segments of Britain and will soon have its impact on America unless the Church perceives the danger of her lifeless ways and repents, crying for a restoration of our dry bones. Still another emerging church leader has been labeled **"the next Billy Graham"** by the *Chicago Sun-Times*. After all – the Media knows! That leader said: **"We're rediscovering Christianity as an Eastern religion."** This statement denies the Westward move of the Gospel as conducted by the Holy Spirit for almost two thousand years!

To my knowledge every leader in the emerging church believes there are other ways to God besides Jesus. He may be the best way, but not the only way, they would tell us. **The emerging church, by returning to ancient mystic practices, teaches that anyone – Christian and non-Christian alike – can tune into God and the spiritual world.**

God loves people, but He hates any religion that offers false hope to those who seek The false religion of the East favors gods whose only power is evil, demonic spirits. Eastern gods cannot save—and those who follow them reject Jesus Christ, the only One who can save. It is just and right that God should hate those who hate His Son; those who turn people away from Jesus Christ, the only One who can save. Our attitude toward the gods of the East should be the same as God's attitude.

In his book, **A Time of Departing,** Ray Yungen reports on the ancient Hindu practice called Kundalini Energy that is currently invading the Christian Church. [Yungen's book is available at **http//www. lighthousetrails.com**.] When a seeker journeys into contemplative prayer he comes to a "still point" which may be defined as a time and place where the mind ceases to function. This should be a warning to the Church – especially its leadership! When a seeker finds mental prayer to be unproductive, he may switch off the mind in contemplative prayer, creating a mental passivity. Unbeknown to the seeker, this makes room for demonic activity. One devotee, in Yungen's book, describes what happened: **"Then came the lights! The gold swirls that I had noted on occasion began to intensify, forming themselves into patterns that both intrigued and captivated me . . . They came through complete passivity and only after I had been in the silence for a while."** He then sensing wise sayings coming into his mind and felt he was receiving messages from another. While in the **"still point"** he felt prickly sensations on the top of his head with **"higher levels of concentrated meditation."**

The spiritually alert Christian will sense the dangers throughout the above experience, which the experimenter may feel was innocent enough – but is not! Whenever we seek for a spiritual experience outside of Jesus Christ we place ourselves in a vulnerable position. That cannot be blamed on another! The contemplative prayer method, in addition to mythology, paganism, Gnosticism, mysticism, liberalism, modernism and evolution, all find free expression in the emerging church. The next decade – if America should last so long – will reveal the cost to the true Church for having tried to blend Truth with error. Paul appropriately asks: *"What fellowship has light with darkness? . . ."* And then advises us to *"come out from among them, says the Lord."* [2 Cor. 6:14-7:1] There is no equivocation in the warning of Jesus: *"Beware of false prophets who come to you in sheep's clothing!"* [Mt.7:15] You know the rest of the verse.

It bears repeating: The Great Awakening was vital to Colonial culture; primarily because it instilled a deep reverence for Jesus Christ. Some may not have believed exactly as you or I, but they had a sense of the Lordship and authority of Jesus Christ. This was not only true within church walls: It saturated Colonial culture. As a result of the Spirit of God flooding the country with His presence, Colonial Americans **were committed to never offend Jesus Christ!**

It is not enough for the emergent leaders to give up their emergent practices, be they contemplative prayers, labyrinths or Gnostic foolishness. The promise is firm: *"And you will seek Me and find Me when you search for Me with all your heart."* [Jeremiah 29:13] The absence of a particular sin or heresy does not make one a Christian. Jesus Christ must be given His rightful due! He is Lord of all!

The Great Awakening exposed Rights and Freedoms lying dormant and unclaimed. Early Colonial preachers – followed by the leaders of the Great Awakening found a Liberty in Jesus Christ that no Government could grant nor take away. They walked in the presence of God. No civil government could force them to receive that Liberty; and no civil authority could rend it from them. Theirs was the Liberty Peter knew when told by Jewish leaders not to preach. He boldly said: *"Whether it is right in the sight of God to give heed to you rather than to God, you be the judge. For we cannot but speak the things which we have seen and heard."*[125] With that testimony Peter revealed that God was his final authority and he was duty bound to obey Him! The man overwhelmed with God's presence enjoys His authority and joyfully yields to His will.

We make a grave mistake when we lower God to the level of a buddy, a pal, a chum; one who doesn't take sin too seriously. Jesus Christ is not an experience to be found in some mystical practice. He is a person to be known, honored and respected as the Eternal King.

When the White Haven Congregational Church wanted to revise their creed in 1788, they called on a stalwart member, Roger Sherman, a signer of the Declaration of Independence as well as the Constitution, to do the revision. Here are but a couple sentences of Sherman's wisdom found in that creed: **I believe that there is one only living and true God, existing in three persons, the Father, the Son, and the Holy Ghost, the same in substance equal in power and glory. That the scriptures of the old and new testaments are a revelation from God, and a complete rule to direct us how we may glorify and enjoy Him!** [126] Roger Sherman would not have been tempted by Emergent foolishness!

The facts before us call for soul-searching, prayer and a seeking of God for another Great Awakening. Can these bones live again? Indeed they can! Indeed they can!

SECTION IV –

<u>THE BREATH OF LIFE</u>

W hen God made man in the Garden of Eden, He breathed into him the breath of life, and man became a living soul, capable of communicating with his Creator. He lost that relationship when he chose to be his own god. Jesus came to take us back to the Father.

Peter warns: **"The end of all things is at hand; therefore, be of sound judgment and sober spirit for the purpose of prayer."** [1 Peter 4:7] In the light of America's present condition, it is essential for the believer to be serious-minded – for the purpose of prayer. If we have no clear picture of what God's intention is for America we will have no objective in our prayer life. We are to **be of sound judgment and sober spirit—for the purpose of prayer;** not for the purpose of criticism, disgust or arrogance; but **for prayer.**

Various tribes of Israel became loyal to David when, in God's timing, he was to be their ruler.

Among them were two hundred leaders from the tribe of Issachar along with their men, **"men who understood the times, with knowledge of what Israel should do."** [1 Chronicles 12:32] Those were dark days under King Saul, David's predecessor, when no one understood the situation, and no one knew what to do. How indispensible it was for David to have the men of Issachar on his side; they knew what to do!

As we consider these final chapters on the Providence of God, His Mandates, His Hand and His Judgments, may we know what to do, and know how to pray!

18 – THE PROVIDENCE OF GOD

America!
When you were young, two hundred years ago,
Beset by every circumstance and foe;
You looked to God's kind Providential Hand,
It was your wisdom, causing you to stand.

From o'er the world men braved the open sea;
From tyranny they came for living free.
They found in you God's Liberty in Law,
And it had caused the world to stand in awe.

But you have lost the greatness once you knew;
Prosperity and evil you pursue.
God's Providence you laid aside for gain,
And now you stand before your God in shame.

The U.S. Constitution was created in 1787. However, if State ratifying conventions voted against it, the young nation would have died in child birth. There would be no United States. So it fell to Alexander Hamilton, James Madison and John Jay to convince the public that it made good sense to ratify the new Document. In a series of 85 articles that appeared in New York newspapers, these men laid out the wisdom of adopting the Constitution. These articles were then compiled into **The Federalist Papers**. John Jay wrote in #2 that **"it was the design of Providence"** that the Colonies be united into one. In #37 James Madison marveled in the coming together of the Colonies into a single unit. He said:

"It is impossible for the man of pious reflection not to perceive in it a finger of that Almighty hand which has been so frequently extended to our relief in the critical stages of the revolution."[127]

Providence was the most vital component in Early America, even more than responsibility, morality or unity. To the modern mind, Providence no longer applies or even exists. Man runs his own affairs; everything can be explained in human terms. Like the rationalist who is sure he can give a good explanation for every life-changing conversion to Christ ever recorded. We need not labor the point further: A miracle is a miracle; and Providence is Providence. It is as sure as *"Jesus Christ is the same yesterday and today and forever"* and that He is also *"a Rewarder of those who seek Him."* [Hebrews 13:8; 11:6] Arguments may blot it from the minds of men but cannot purge it from reality.

The word Providence is derived from the Latin, *providentia*, which means **the act of preparing for future application.** Webster's 1828 Dictionary says that Providence is **the care God exercises over his creatures.** Adding that **a general providence consists of particulars! A belief in divine providence is a source of great consolation to good men.** The Providence that brought America into existence is the Providence that continues to sustain America. When that Providence is withdrawn America can do nothing to prevent collapse.

The Providence of God is not merely a personal point of view; it is a Biblical truth. Colossians 1:16-17 tells us that *Jesus Christ created all things, both in heaven and on earth, visible and invisible, whether thrones, dominions, rulers or authorities—all things were created by Him and for Him. And He is before all things, and in Him all things consist and hold together.* The following verse tells us that *"He is also the Head of the Church,"* which phrase carries a subsidiary truth to the main Truth: Providence rules ALL!

Naturalists do not like the idea that anyone other than himself runs the world. Man feels that somehow things cannot function without his hand on the wheel. That which is our duty – like the economy – we do not do very well. That which is not our role – global-warming or global-cooling – we think we are the only ones with solutions, for the God who created the world is no longer around to sustain it. Providence will handle nature very well – if we are faithful to Him. The naturalist tells us nature created all things, and where it might go awry man can fix it. All this striving is man's attempt to eliminate Providence from the world. How foolish!

When Jesus Christ stepped down from Glory into this world and began His earthly ministry, the whole religious world was upset. He brought with Him Providence, revealing the true nature of God. In the Old Testament, God was involved in Israel's life at Mount Sinai with thundering and lightening, the Ten Commandments and the Old Covenant. In the New Testament – the New Covenant – God was in Christ with compassion, grace and truth. [John 1:14.17; 2 Cor.5:19] Here in Jesus Christ, the *__Divine Providentia__* was revealed to the world!

In America's beginnings Providence was not merely a theory; it was reality. Since we have removed God – as much as possible – from our consciousness, He is no longer appreciated. He, or anyone representing Him, is unwanted in our self-confident, man-controlled existence. Psalm 2:1-3 describes this conflict: *"The nations . . . the peoples . . . the kings . . . the rulers, all take counsel together against God and His Anointed One, Jesus Christ, saying, we will not have this One to reign over us."*

Due to its passive attitude, the Church hesitates to challenge the naturalist or modernist. Instead, Church leaders choose to listen to them, for they might have some wisdom to add to our ignorance. Some years ago I took a refresher course at a Seminary near Portland, Oregon. We were studying a liberal book that explained away all the miracles and demonic deliverances in the earthly ministry of Jesus. The author's intention was to convince the reader that Jesus was simply an ordinary man with extraordinary influence over people. A young student with three years of Bible College confessed: **"I can't say that Jesus is real, like I know this table is real."** To which I said, **"If you have ever met Jesus Christ you'll know He's more real than this table!"** Uncertainty is the heart of Liberal Education! Professors like students who are ever learning and never able to come to the knowledge of the Truth [2 Tim.3:7]. For the teacher who says, **"We can never know anything for sure!"** There is but one question: **"Are you sure?"**

God made man in the Garden of Eden and though man rebelled, God still longs to bless and care for him. Here we see a perpetual tension between God's Providence and His Righteousness! He cannot look with approval on sin due to His innate Righteousness. It was for this reason God put man out of the Garden and out of His presence. God is Righteous; He cannot look on sin – but He is also Providence and Compassion! Therefore, He finds a way, not to eliminate His Righteousness in order to meet man on a corrupt level; but He finds a way to satisfy His Righteous nature: He becomes guilty of man's guilt. Jesus takes the sin of the world upon Himself and suffers a shameful death on our behalf: *"He, who knew no sin, became sin for us . . ."* [2 Cor.5:21 Such is the Hand of Providence: Mercy satisfies the Righteous nature of God while meeting Man's need forgiveness! Every person who comes to Jesus Christ to be forgiven can be certain of two things: First, that Jesus will receive any who come to Him; and second, He will purify all who come. He will leave no one spiritually soiled in His Kingdom.

Without the Hand of Providence there would be no America. This country was not an accident; nor did it develop by the wisdom of man. It is Providence that made us what we are today, causing the U.S. Supreme Court to say in 1892, **". . . this is a Christian nation."** And say in 1931, **"We are a Christian people . . . and acknowledge with reverence the duty of obedience to the will of God."**[128]

Are all nations equal? What makes a nation Righteous? First, we understand that an individual person is only made Righteous through Jesus Christ. When Jesus comes into a person's life He brings with Him His character, His Spirit, His Righteousness. By nature *there is none Righteous, no not one!* [Romans 3:10] Since the Garden of Eden, everyone who ever got right with God did so by grace, not by works or any other means. Nations, on the other hand, are Righteous according to their alliance with the Law of Nature as well as the Revealed Law of God as found in Christian Scripture. While individuals can and must repent of disobedience to the will of God, nations cannot repent: But they can – if there are enough godly folks in the land – to get back into line with the will of God. A nation is headed by its Government: That Government must submit itself to its proper role: If it does not the Hand of Providence is withheld. If it acknowledges Jesus Christ as the proper head of all *"thrones, dominions, rulers or authorities* – which requires humility – it will surely know the Hand of Providence in its defense, in its prosperity and in its progress among the nations of the world. [See Col.1:16-17]

It is beautiful indeed to see the Hand of Providence in nature. Volumes have been written on the topic; we consider it briefly: Animals do not rebel; they simply live up to their wild or domesticated natures. Year after year they follow instincts installed by God: He taught the birds not to lay eggs in the wintertime. And to sit on eggs until they hatch. God taught the mother bird how and what to feed its helpless chicks; and the hummingbird to fly across the Gulf of Mexico, a distance of 450 miles, and return again the following spring, reaching New Orleans in February, Central Missouri in March, Green Bay in April, and Canada in May – year after year – year after year. Before they make their flight they first gain up to 40% of their body weight. Who told them to do that? Who told them which way to go – and when? Who told geese to hatch their young in the Arctic just when there is an endless supply of newly hatched mosquitoes for their goslings to eat? I recall on our Southern Wisconsin farm how we had a chicken sit on duck eggs, but she was totally confused when they hatched. She may have been bothered by their odd appearance, but was frantic when without hesitation they jumped into the pond. She ran around, calling them – but they refused to leave the water. How does a mother chicken know to keep young chicks out of the water? Because a newly-hatched chick will immediately drown! Who taught that to the mother hen? A thousand other aspects are explained and answered only by Providence. [See Job 39-42] But there is more to Providence than the care of hummingbirds and goslings. It is **the care and superintendence which God exercises over man.** Webster adds that **"the same power which caused a thing to exist is necessary to continue its existence.** Providence is the foundation upon which America was built.

We cannot expect the Culture [Commerce, Labor, Arts, Media, etc,] to move American society back to its rightful foundation, the Bible. Nor can we expect Government to do so, for Government is like rabbits and dandelions: More concerned with multiplying its own than recognizing its duty to serve the citizens and obey God's Laws. This being so, the Church must step forward – not with programs and plans but with a call to repent and turn back to the simple yet all-inclusive Declaration of Independence. God will work with the Church – if the Church will work with God – in God's way – to bring about a new Awakening. Obviously, *"it is time for judgment to begin with the household of God."* [1 Peter 4:17] We cannot call the Culture and Government to correction unless the Church itself experiences the Intense Presence of Jesus Christ.

Sodom was destroyed because God could not find ten Righteous people in the city [Genesis 18:10; 19:29]. When it becomes more Righteous for God to destroy America than to preserve it, neither arms nor negotiations will prevail. Until then – as long as there are Righteous in the land – the Hand of Providence reigns and the Church awaits the fresh breath of God.

19 – THE MANDATES OF GOD

A mandate is a directive from a superior to an inferior. It is an authorization from one who is legally qualified to give orders. It is an edict by one sufficiently powerful to enforce the edict. As the term is used here, Divine Mandate refers to a divinely imposed task. It is Divine inasmuch as it is authorized by the Son of God, whose authority is beyond question.

There are four such Mandates in Christian Scriptures: Culture, Government, Family and Church. All four are directly accountable to Jesus Christ. The Church is to speak righteousness to the other three, but has no controlling authority. Some assume that, because Jesus Christ and the Church are intimately united, the Church is to control Government. Others have assumed the Church should have power over the Family, even suggesting who and when to marry. Control was assumed by the Roman Church when it was united with the Roman Empire beginning with Emperor Constantine: It was a union unauthorized in Scripture.

Jesus Christ is God! All truths hinge on this all-inclusive Truth! Scriptures confirm this undeniable fact: Not only did the disciple Thomas acknowledge Jesus Christ as God [John 20:28], the Heavenly Father Himself said to Jesus: *"Thy throne, O God, is forever and ever!"* [Hebrews 1:8] And Paul told Timothy that Jesus Christ is *the only wise God.* [1 Tim.1:17] This being true, He has the authority to issue Mandates for the carrying out of His plans for the world and man.

The Four Mandates are: **1 - Government** – the oversight of civil matters by leaders. **2 - Family** – designed in the Garden of Eden – Adam and his wife Eve – with eventual children – a purpose backed by the Law of Moses and blessed by Jesus Christ. **3 - Culture** – including labor, commerce, the arts, etc., was designed for the development of the natural world for the comfort and blessing of mankind. **4 - The Church** – where Jesus Christ resides and His message is proclaimed.

The Four Mandates are under the direct rule of Jesus Christ. None of them rule each other! Dietrich Bonhoeffer warns that there is no basis **"for any kind of domination of the Church over the government, or the government over the family, or of culture over government or Church, or of any other overlordship which may be thought in this connexion."**[129] Bonhoeffer is Biblical here. However, both Dominion Theology and Liberation Theology and Black Liberation Theology disagree. These are beyond the scope of this book, but a brief remark is in order: [1] Dominion Theology says the Church is to take dominion over demons, the devil, etc. This is not Biblical for the Scripture says to submit to God and resist the devil and he will flee from you [James 4:7]. The enemy is to be treated with resistance, not taking mastery over him. [2] Liberation Theology says the Church is to have dominion over the institutions of the world. This is not Biblical either, for each of the Four Mandates is under the direct authority of Jesus Christ; none are under the control or dominion of any of the other three. [3] Black Liberation Theology, as taught by James Cone and Michael Wright and believed by perhaps one quarter of Black pastors, assert that Jesus Christ is Black and that He came to set the Blacks free from social, political, economic and religious oppression by the White establishment.

Each of these theologies is a divergent system. Men are keen on using God for personal ends. Our goal as people of God is to see that we do not stand in His way; that we observe and cooperate with what Providence is about. Jesus Christ Himself has dominion over the world's institutions, though they might think otherwise.

Christians often relegate Jesus to the past – He once lived! Providence no longer applies to our modern world. At the same time we readily consign Him to the distant future – He will return some day! He presently reigns, doing so through Four Mandates, ruling over the affairs of men in a world that was created by Him and for Him. Jesus Christ Himself ordered the installation and function of these Mandates. This is seen in Colossians 1:15-17 where Paul tells us Jesus Christ *created all things* and *by Him all things hold together,* as well as many other Scriptures. [See Mt.28:18-20; Jn.1:1-3; Heb.1:1-2]

Regarding the Church's message, Bonhoeffer writes: **"The Church's word derives its sole right and its sole authority from the commission of Christ, and consequently any word which she may utter without reference to this authority will be devoid of all significance."**[130] The reference to Christ's Commission is found in Matthew 28:18ff, where the Church is instructed to go into the world and teach all nations. It is also found in Acts 26:16ff, where Paul is commissioned to be the servant of Jesus. This same commission is applicable to all servants of Christ: We are here to **open the spiritual eyes of the blind; turn them from darkness to light and from the power of Satan unto God, so they receive forgiveness of sins.**

The ministry of the Church is tri-directional: Toward God, toward itself and toward the world. The Church is to worship God and serve only Him. He is the Church's only Master: There is none other! Second, the Church is to minister to itself, building each other up in faith and love, through counsel and prayer overlaid with compassion. Third, the Church is to call sinners to repentance and faith. **The church is not authorized to create a utopia here on earth**, despite what the prosperity preacher told you! The Church has certain parameters inside of which it is to function. Whenever it steps outside of those bounds — though it invariably sells a feel-good message – it loses its spiritual life and authority: The Spirit is under no obligation to be present anywhere Jesus Christ is not given His rightful place. **He does not bless opinions**, however nicely they are framed; He will, however, consistently bear witness to the truth.

None of the Four Mandates is spun off into the world to function on its own. To the measure that any of the Four become independent from Jesus Christ – the One who ordained their existence – to that measure it loses the wisdom and power to fulfill its God-chosen purpose. Paul tells us in Colossians 1:17

that Jesus Christ sustains all things: If He is rejected, dismissed or simply forgotten, and any of the Four Mandates expect to function without Him, they inevitably deteriorate and fail. Dietrich Bonhoeffer points out that these Four Mandates **are 'for' one another; otherwise they are not God's mandates.** Inasmuch as Government was ordained by God, its role is to support the moral law of God; defend the Church's right to freely worship; see that commerce and labor are free to function for the betterment of citizens; as well as defend the traditional family and the Inalienable Rights of its citizenry.

During Colonial days, Government and the laws of the land were godly. Consequently, when a man did wrong against the law of God he could not flee to Government for protection. Today – as in the case of adultery, abortion, pornography, sodomy and homosexuality, government defends the sinner and protects him from being convicted by the Spirit of God. This was not so in Colonial America. At that time the sinner had nowhere to flee – except into the arms of Jesus for forgiveness, deliverance and Liberty.

When any of the Four Mandates drifts away from the authority of Jesus Christ, they seek an alternative authority under which to function: **Government** becomes Statism, where it becomes a man-run and man-organized system, determining right and wrong without God. **Family**, a creation of God, was neither a product of society nor a decision by Government. God made them male and female: This is a major aspect of the Law of Nature installed at the time of creation.

When society becomes Self-absorbed it moves toward divorce or some divergent and self-centered lifestyle – and in the process seeks the protection of Government for its sin. **Culture**, as it yields to the Law of Nature, finds Freedom in Self-Government, which habitually leads to free-market capitalism. When it fails to observe the Law of Nature it becomes Socialistic and then Communistic: Government-owned and State-controlled. A free Culture leads to prosperity. Government contributes nothing. When it grows beyond control, it eats up the profits Culture creates. **Church**, built by Jesus Christ and added to by His primary agent, the Holy Spirit, consists of the Body of believers. When it ceases to follow Jesus Christ it becomes organizational, man-controlled, institutional and stagnant. The institution becomes primarily concerned with making a name for itself. It adopts social programs, becoming increasingly concerned with man's earthly comforts rather than man's personal rightness with God. Neither bigness nor activity are proofs that the Church is pleasing God. Usually the opposite! This is called liberalism!

Each of the Four Mandates was created by Jesus Christ and for Jesus Christ. Government is assigned the task of maintaining and protecting the other Mandates, but it did not create them. Government has no creative power. Marriage, Labor and the Church have their origin in God; they were not established by Government, which has the role of protector, not controller.

The Church is especially dear to the heart of Jesus Christ, even pictured in Scripture as the Bride of

Christ. The present organization, called the church, has bonded with many other suitors and lovers, while the Bridegroom awaits the devotion of His Bride. The modern organizational church is a product of the will and wit of man, functioning under an alternative authority – man. Sadder still is that few recognize the problem. The bones are indeed dry, in need of the Breath of God!

> John tells us of Jesus Christ's rightful place in Revelation 4:11: *"Thou art worthy, O Lord, to receive glory and honor and power: For Thou hast created all things, and for Thy pleasure they are and were created."*

Although the Colonists did not label these Four Mandates as such, there is nothing in our research that would tell us they failed in any of the Four. As for **Government**, Jonathan Edwards writes of a time when there will be *"peace and love between rulers and ruled. Rulers shall love their people, and with all their might seek their best good; and the people shall love their rulers, and . . . give them that honor which is their due."*[131] How times have changed since George Washington was joyously inaugurated our First President on April 30, 1789. Washington was a President who did not strive for the office, and yet served America and the cause of Freedom most worthily. [Note: A word is in order regarding President George Bush: From the outset the media despised his Christianity; they maligned him. Christians, instead of standing firm, fearfully cowered in the corner lest someone ask if they support Bush. But we ask: Which of his decisions violated the Law of Nature or the U.S. Constitution? We tend to listen to the opinions of the media, not the voice of the Spirit. Has the Church failed here? I believe so! In this rebuke, I include myself.]

As for the **Family**, divorce happened in Colonial America, but seldom. This was also true of abortions. Dr. Bernard Nathanson was a leader in the fight for legalizing abortion before the U.S. Supreme Court in 1973. He personally fed the media the idea that there were 10,000 illegal abortions in back alleys prior to Roe v Wade. Since his "conversion," Nathanson admits that the 10,000 figure was made up by him; that the actual figure was around 200 to 250. He recently said, *"As a scientist I know . . . that human life begins at conception."*[132] The traditional Family is God's plan, not to be changed by legislative action or judicial decision. It is worth noting that a Man and a Woman cannot create a child; they make a child from the ingredients provided to them by the Creator.

As America shifts more and more from a Conservative base to a Liberal base, there is a corresponding shift in the culture's attitude toward life. **"Life begins at conception!"** If not, what other time could it be? Liberals may insist that the issue is much broader than abortion: They insist we must consider **the Common Good:** Such as starving children, inadequate health insurance, people without jobs, the environment, and a host of other people-related issues. While looking at the big picture we cast aside the tiny baby. The Supreme Court may say we have no way of knowing when life begins, as they said in Roe v Wade, but the involuntary muscles begin to develop the moment of conception. All the elements of personhood are there, though not yet mature. It is a serious thing for a parent to destroy the living baby in the womb; it is dreadfully criminal and a violation of God's Law of Nature for the death of a child to be sanctioned by man-made laws.

Commerce in Colonial times was obviously simple; trading was prominent. As the Colonies grew the economy grew. Laws were minimal – perhaps that can be attributed at least in part to the distinctive Christian culture. Today it is quite different: Every facet of business, commerce and labor is under governmental scrutiny. Perhaps that is because Americans are no longer self-governed. As more laws are created with the intention of keeping everyone in line, the people increasingly seek ways to circumvent those laws – which makes it necessary to create still more laws. Hundreds of laws are enacted annually by federal, state and local governments. Human laws are designed to keep us from being bad and protect us from ourselves. Even God does not do that: His laws are designed to grant us the Freedom to err and then pay the price through natural consequences for any infraction.

Marriage and Commerce have their origins in God. He created them both in the Garden of Eden. Adam was to be joined to his wife Eve; and Adam was to care for the Garden. Neither of the two was established by Government. As soon as Government is formed – because it is composed of men – it immediately seeks ways to exercise control. Of the Four Mandates, the one most likely to exceed its role is Government; it has the legislators, the army, the police, the courts, and the whole bureaucratic machine at its disposal to take control beyond its rightful place assigned by God. That is called tyranny. Bonhoeffer writes that *"it is only in protecting the righteous that government fulfils its true mission of serving Christ."*[133] William Penn, the founder of Pennsylvania, told Peter the Great, Czar of Russia, in a letter: *"If thou wouldst rule well, thou must rule for God, and to do that, thou must be ruled by Him . . ."*[134]

Imagine what it might be like if there was another Great Awakening when, as Jonathan Edwards tells us that *rulers love their people, and seek their best good; and the people love their rulers.* What a glorious day that would be! No more would it be necessary for citizens to fight for Inalienable Rights, for Government would understand and would stand with citizens in the defense of those Rights. No more would Government impose unbiblical and government-created, civil rights on the people as though they were God-ordered and Inalienable. Only a Great spiritual Awakening wherein the presence of God reigns will bring about such a world. The question remains as to whether society – or even the present-day Church – would want such a one as the Son of God to reign. For example, one day a man came to Jesus and said: **"Tell my brother to divide the inheritance with me!"** Jesus answered: **"Who**

appointed Me a judge or arbiter over you?" Then Jesus added: **"Beware of covetousness: A man's life does not consist in the abundance of things he accumulates!"** [Luke 12:13-15] Many prayer requests on our prayer chains seek covetous answers which, if I understand Jesus, He does not answer. He is not our servant; we are His, having been bought with His blood. What would Jesus do? We cannot know – until we bow at His feet in absolute submission!

John Adams, our 2nd President, said: *"Suppose a nation in some distant region should take the Bible for their only law book, and every member should regulate his conduct by the precepts there exhibited! Every member would be obliged in conscience, to temperance, frugality, and industry; to justice, kindness, and charity towards his fellow men; and to piety, love and reverence toward Almighty God. . . What a Eutopia, what a Paradise would this be.*"[135]

As for the **Church**, it is the treasure hidden in the field, the world! To gain that treasure, Jesus sells all that He has, giving up the presence of His Father, in order to buy the world to get the treasure – the Church, to own it and maintain it as His own [See Mt.13:44]. Consider Christ's evaluations of the Church: A **Bride** adorned for her Husband; a **Branch** attached to the Vine; **Sheep** tenderly cared for by the Good Shepherd; a **Temple** indwelt by the Spirit of God.

The nature of America was spiritual in Colonial days! We cannot attempt to impulsively and by sheer will-power take America back to what it once was. Dietrich Bonhoeffer warned that *fanaticism* ends in failure. The fanatic, he writes, *"inevitably ends by tiring and admitting defeat. . . He will sooner or later become entangled with non-essentials and petty details and fall into the snare set by his more skilful opponent."*[136]

Passivity – the opposite of *fanaticism* – is likewise unacceptable to Christ: It leaves the Christian lifeless, spiritless and useless to the Savior. The answer: Present ourselves without hesitation or fear to God, and thereby *"reveal that good, acceptable and perfect will of God."* [Romans 12:1-2] Inasmuch as Jesus Christ was totally committed to us, we should demand no less of ourselves. This is not a frightening requirement: It is the only place of peace and protection by the God of Providence.

Every person is subject to these Four Mandates: He is to support and defend them; never war against them. The first three – Government, Family and Commerce – do not require Christian conversion for the citizen to participate. The Church, however, requires the New Birth as the entrance point. [John 3:1-5] The Church is composed of those who have been converted to faith in Jesus Christ. The Church is the body of believers who know and love God. They are those whose guilt has been borne away by Jesus Christ Himself; they know it and more importantly: God knows it. As a result the believer has become God's messenger; the voice of God to address issues when the spiritual backbone needs alignment and brought back in accord with God's design. We should know the will of God. The Church, because she personally knows the Master, senses the Master's will in regard to the Four Mandates. Wherever we think we have a perfect handle on the will of God, however, we fall into the trap of ___*fanaticism*___ in attempting to straighten out the Mandate upon which we have fixed our attention.

In addition to knowing God's purposes for the Culture, Family and Government, the Pastor and the Church exist in the world to issue the call to know and follow Jesus Christ. That call came to Levi, also called Matthew, in Mark 2:14. When Jesus saw him in his tax office Jesus simply said *"Follow Me!"* That was all that was needed, and Levi *"rose and followed Him."* Here is the matchless authority of Jesus Christ, the Son of God.

1 – We have no record of any preliminaries; just *"Follow Me!"* and Levi follows.

2 – The reason for Levi's following is singular: **Jesus!** No other reason is given.

3 – Jesus asks no confession of Levi; like, *"Do you confess that it was sin to collect taxes?"*

4 – Levi is not praised for following: Being in the presence of Jesus is reward enough!

5 – Levi is not asked to develop a Purpose-Driven program; just *follow Me! You do not know the way – but I do!*

6 – Levi has no security—except Jesus! He knows not what tomorrow will bring.

7 – From now on Levi has no freedom to do his own thing: He is free only to please Jesus!

8 – Levi gets no clear instructions regarding his life's work. Simply: *"Follow Me!"*

We too need to first hear that call ourselves and follow Jesus Christ. He has an undeniable drawing power. No other religion has a divine Savior. All the rest entice or persuade people to do the best they can to follow their leader, but Jesus, with a simple call compels our hearts to love and follow Him. With these simple words – *Follow Me* – Levi is absolutely changed from pursuing his own agenda to having no agenda, save Jesus alone! Jesus the Son of God has the power to change us so that we come to life as surely and as promptly as Ezekiel's dry bones. **"God, who is rich in mercy, because of His great love with which He loves us, even when we were dead in our sins, made us alive in Christ."** [Eph.2:4-5] There is no greater joy on earth! Who would not follow Christ, the only One who has such love?

20 – THE HAND OF GOD

In 1976, the late Dr. Francis Schaeffer produced a video series and book entitled: *__How Should We Then Live__*. According to Schaeffer the battle is fought out on the stage of human history. That being so—we are each a part of that struggle! We would rather think that every situation turns out comfortable – but such is not the case.

Dietrich Bonhoeffer is an example of a man who knew the Hand of God on his life. He tells us – **"only the man who is dead to his own will can follow Christ."** He understood, having been constantly urged to give up his battle against Hitler and sell out to the Nazis like so many others did in 1940s Germany. In *__Ethics__*, Bonhoeffer tells us that both fanaticism and passivity fall before the enemy. The fanatic quickly sees the enemy is bigger than he is; and the passive one ends up defeated by his own conscience for doing nothing. **How should we then live?** We find out as we follow the Hand of God on Bonhoeffer.

World War II began in 1939 while Bonhoeffer was lecturing in America. What he said in one of his lectures still presses on us today: ". . . **Christians in Germany will face the terrible alternative of either willing the defeat of their nation in order that Christian civilization may survive, or willing the victory of their nation and thereby destroying our civilization! I know which of these alternatives I must choose; but I cannot make this choice in security."**[137] Bonhoeffer was compelled to leave the security of America, considering complacency **a great sin against the Holy Spirit**. He also regarded **self-ambition a part of the road to hell**. He must return: The survival of Germany was at stake.

But what could one man do? How could Bonhoeffer expect to be effective against Hitler and his mighty war machine that was, unless God intervened, about to master all of Europe, including her churches, social institutions, the youth, the armies, and every home and family? So what could one insignificant preacher expect to do in the face of such odds? The size of Goliath would not deter David: Bonhoeffer returned to Germany—into the teeth of the lion.

In *Memoir*, written as a preface to Bonhoeffer's *The Cost of Discipleship*, G. Leibholz writes that steadfastness of mind and willingness to sacrifice all in obedience to Christ was characteristic of Bonhoeffer. For example, when in 1940, many were seized by the Gestapo [**Ge**rman **Sta**te **Po**lice], and many others began to indicate a willingness to capitulate, Bonhoeffer said **"If we claim to be Christians, there is no room for expediency."**[138] The group of Christians he led went right on with their anti-Hitler activities, despite those inside and outside of Germany who believed a total Nazi victory was inevitable. Later, when the question arose as to who would inform the British government of their continued struggle, Bonhoeffer volunteered in the face of extreme danger.

Brought in for interrogation in May of 1942 Bonhoeffer refused to change his position, defying the Gestapo machine by openly admitting that, as a Christian, he was a relentless enemy of National Socialism. He was threatened with torture as well as threats to arrest his parents, his sisters and his fiancée, but he stood firm. Today – in the early 2000s – we are increasingly faced with the same socialistic plans for America. With our American Declaration of Independence and Constitution so clearly anti-socialistic, a politician for national office will not announce that he is a socialist—until we are at the point of no return. Our opposition to socialism must be like the firmness of Bonhoeffer!

In April, 1943, Bonhoeffer was imprisoned! The following year his friends found a way for him to escape and be shuttled to safety abroad. He refused, staying in prison lest his escape endanger others. Furthermore, he had a ministry to fellow-prisoners and to Nazi guards, many of whom came to faith in Christ because of his radiant witness.

Those in prison with Bonhoeffer could move about freely – except at night when they were shackled. However, because of the ministry Bonhoeffer had toward the other prisoners, there were times when he was not shackled because he was trusted; he was left free to minister to anxious prisoners and guards. One of those fellow prisoners was a British Captain by the name of Payne Best who, after liberation, wrote of Bonhoeffer: **". . . without exception the finest and most lovable man I ever met . . . at perfect ease . . . his soul shone in the dark, desperation of our prison . . . we were in complete agreement**

that our guards needed pity far more than we . . ."[139]

Hans von Dohnanyi was married to Christine, Bonhoeffer's sister. Dohnanyi served as the legal advisor for the resistance movement against Hitler and was also imprisoned with Bonhoeffer in 1943. In a letter smuggled out in a Thermos flask, Dohnanyi wrote to his wife Christine: **"What you have been and are to me and to the children could have made me one of the happiest men under God's sun. Still, I believe we were right to worry about the fate of others, which is what makes one become political."**[140]

It is encouraging to have the support and encouragement of friends and the Church when trials increase. Such was not the case in Germany where only a few saw the vile heart of Hitler for what it was. Those who did see the wickedness determined there was nothing that could be done about it. Rudolf Brettscheid, leader of the Social Democrats, rejoiced in 1933 when he heard Hitler was named chancellor, believing Hitler would now be exposed for what he really was.[141] Little did Brettscheid and other capitulators realize the deceit and depravity of Hitler's mind as he gathered men around him to secure his place of power. Joachim Fest compares the Nazi movement to other movements, saying, **"Like all other mass movements, the Nazi movement owed at least some of its dynamism and vigor to this widespread desire for change."**[142] Change: Where have we heard that before?

Few appreciated the rowdy lawlessness that developed among the German youth while Hitler was solidifying his reign: They were sure the powerful and charismatic Hitler would take care of that shortly. They did not realize Hitler would soon use rowdy young people to his advantage: They would be called upon to inform on pastors, friends, neighbors, fellow-students and co-workers. Their reward would be prestige and status in the Nazi party for turning in anyone, including their own parents, who questioned Hitler's intentions!

Unity in the Protestant Church against Hitler gradually crumbled. The typical tradition in Lutheranism was to yield to the authority of the state, seeking an arrangement with the government so they might continue to function normally. A few, like Pastor Martin Niemoller and Dietrich Bonhoeffer, saw through Hitler's deceptive heart and refused to yield, paying for their insight with prison sentences. One after another of Hitler's foes were brought to their knees before the Fuhrer. Though there were 24 major conspirators against Hitler, and most of them were church members of some sort, Pastor Bonhoeffer stood quite alone in the spiritual end of the battle.

A month or so before the end of the war Hitler knew he could not win. He had long forgotten the glorious history of the Reformation that had changed Germany and much of Europe. Now, Hitler would conquer the lands once touched by Martin Luther. But America was advancing on Berlin from the West, and the Soviets from the East. At that point Hitler was sure he would have conquered all of Europe, perhaps even Asia, had it not been for Bonhoeffer and his conspirator friends. There was one thing to do: have Heinrich Himmler, head of the Gestapo, order the deaths of Bonhoeffer and his friends.

Dietrich Bonhoeffer was never tried: The verdict was not open for appeal! The day before his hanging on April 9, 1945, Bonhoeffer held his final Church service with many of his fellow prisoners and with the Lord, for Jesus had said, *where two or three are gathered in My name, there I am!* [Mt.18:20] Bonhoeffer was not fretful about his upcoming death; rather, he was concerned with the wives of inmates that they might be free from anxiety. At the end of the service Gestapo officers took Bonhoeffer to Flossenburg prison for hanging the following morning. As he parted from his friends he said: **"This is the end . . . but for me it is the beginning of life!"**[143]

We have no record of Dietrich Bonhoeffer's thoughts during the night before his hanging. Might he have wondered: **If only I had stayed in America six years ago!** Or: **If only I had let them help me escape when I had the chance!** Or: **Why did I ever get involved in this worthless operation?** But we have no such record. Having studied Bonhoeffer's life of enthusiastic devotion to Jesus Christ, we can clearly say: Dietrich Bonhoeffer had no such regrets; he faced death with courage!

The German doctor on duty at Flossenburg gives us the following report: **Between five and six o'clock in the morning, Canaris, Oster, Dr. Sack** and Pastor Bonhoeffer, were taken from their cells and the verdict read to them. Through the half-open door of his cell, I had seen the pastor kneeling in prayer. I have never before been so moved. His devotion was absolute; he appeared almost cheerful. Later, in front of the gallows, he repeated a short prayer and then climbed up to the rope with complete composure. He was dead in a few seconds. During my fifty years' experience in medicine, I have never seen anyone die so calmly and so trustingly.[144]

Adolf Hitler had prayed for Germany's victory over all of Europe. A few temporary successes he took to be Divine Providence; such as the time a suitcase bomb was exploded in the Fuhrer's bunker: Though he was injured, his life was spared, and he declared his safety to be the work of Providence.

Dietrich Bonhoeffer also prayed – not for Hitler's success but for American victory. We know whose prayers were answered. While Allied forces are given credit for setting Europe free from Hitler's planned domination, how much effect the prayers of Bonhoeffer had is only known in Heaven. Who was it that sent the snows that bogged down the German troops on the Russian Front? Was it not the Hand of Providence? Who was it that split the clouds on an overcast day over the coast of France so hundreds of Allied planes could parachute in thousands of men for the invasion of Normandy? We will not know this side of glory how much these – and many other providential events – were answers to the prayers of Bonhoeffer.

Francis Schaeffer counsels: **"The primary battle is a spiritual battle in the heavenlies,"** adding that **"the heavenly battle is fought on the stage of human history."**[145] Bonhoeffer's stage was Flossenburg prison, where he fought and won! Now – the battle is ours! Regardless of our personal future, we face it not as fanatics or passives. We place our hand firmly in the Hand of God as we battle for a wayward nation called America – awaiting and pleading for the breath of God to bring life to dry, lifeless bones.

21 – THE JUDGMENTS OF GOD

Solomon had wealth and wisdom beyond measure: His drinking vessels were of solid gold. His navy brought silver, ivory, gold, apes and peacocks from afar. He had 1400 chariots, 12,000 horsemen and thousands of soldiers who guarded his kingdom. However, God sent marauding bands to harass him because of his sin, but he still did not repent. His kingdom was ultimately divided, and his wealth and wisdom could not save him once the Judgment of God was against him. He chose to violate the Laws of God by letting his many wives bring foreign gods and idols into the very Temple of God at Jerusalem. He needed to confess his sin and seek forgiveness and restoration, but we have no record that he sought the face of God in those last fatal years. He knew how to give good advice to others, saying: **"Remember your Creator in the days of your youth, before the evil days come and you no longer delight in what you once had!"** [Eccl.12:1-2] But he knew not how to live by those words himself. In addition, all Israel suffered because of Solomon's sin. As the leader goes – so goes the nation! This is still true today. To the one who insists that it does not matter who we elect as a leader, consider what happened to Germany due to Hitler's sins, the many that were hanged and the devastation of that nation!

There are two judgments: One of nations and another of persons. Both nations and persons, however, are judged on their relationship and surrender to Jesus Christ, the Ruler of the world.

Nations are to honor Jesus Christ with appreciation for the Four Mandates He installed on earth: They are Government, Culture, Family and the Church. God is not selfish – He did send His Son to die in our place – but Nations will not be allowed to treat God's Beloved Son with disrespect: Those doing so will be judged accordingly. Persons, on the other hand, will be judged on whether they have received Jesus Christ as the Lord and Savior of their lives. Jesus said He was *"the Way,"* and that *"No man comes to the Father but by Me!"* [John 14:6] A serious and conclusive Judgment awaits those who seek salvation through their own goodness or in any other religion or god.

A Nation cannot repent – but Persons, especially those in leadership, are called to repent. Generally, Nations go astray because of unrepentant leadership.

God's judgments are based on Existing Law: This applies to both nations and individuals. Existing Law includes the Law of Nature and the Law of Revelation. Because judgment is based on existing law, a judge's opinion is worthless! All legitimate law is encompassed in this – the Moral Law of God! Nothing can legitimately be called law except Moral Law!

Moral Law is the rule of law that governs all Moral beings. Because man is a Moral being, all laws governing his actions are Moral. It cannot be otherwise. The Moral Law of God, comprising the Law of Nature and the Revealed Law in Scripture, exists for the good of mankind. God loves man – and for that reason Moral Law was authorized.

No one expresses a Nation's duty to Moral Law so concisely and clearly as Lawyer-turned-evangelist Charles G. Finney [1792-1875]. He said **"no government is lawful or innocent that does not recognize the moral law as the only universal law, and God as the Supreme Lawgiver and Judge, to whom nations in their national capacity, as well as all individuals, are amenable. The moral law of God is the only law of individuals and of nations, and nothing can be rightful government but such as is established and administered with a view to its support."**[146] The extent of the hurtful abuse done to Moral Law in America is beyond words, and the consequent harm done to persons is beyond measure. The Judgment to come of Persons and rulers will be on the basis of Existing Moral Law, not on the opinion of judges, liberals or the ACLU.

Animals instinctively obey the Law of Nature: Birds know what and how to feed their young; they instinctively know when chicks are old enough to fend for themselves; and they know when to fly south. They each conduct themselves by built-in natural law. Man is different! He is given reason and a spirit. When spiritually awakened by Jesus Christ to the ways of God, man is changed and conformed to the likeness of Jesus, the Son of God. This is God's goal in His plan of salvation: That we become like Jesus! [Romans 8:29; 12:1-2; 2 Cor. 3:16-18]

As stated earlier, not all God's Judgments of Nations are immediate. Many a leader – like Saul and Solomon and Hezekiah – began under the Providence of God, but ended without it: unprotected and vulnerable. The American experience – to this point in time – is quite like that of Israel. May God deal with us in mercy!

THE RIGHT FORM OF GOVERNMENT

There is one form of Government that is favored by God over other forms. Communists say the future is certain and the past is in doubt. Their reasoning is this: They believe in historic determinism – and historic determinism says Communism is destined to win in the end! The Christian says the opposite: The past is sure but the future is uncertain – because the blessing of God in the future depends on whether we are on God's side. The Communist does not want us to look back, for there he will see on America the blessings of Providence – which he disdains. Communism is totally a man-ordered society, leaving no room for God.

For Communism to take over a country, the groundwork is normally laid by Socialists. Dietrich Bonhoeffer strongly opposed Hitler's brand of Socialism because it not only deprived German citizen's of their rights and freedoms, such as the Freedom to worship [Hitler opposed independent churches] and the Right to life [Hitler killed Bonhoeffer], but it also arbitrarily invaded other sovereign countries. Because Bonhoeffer saw Hitler as a madman, he worked for the defeat of his own country; that, Bonhoeffer said, was the only way

Germany could be delivered from Socialism and return to its Christian roots.

Eventually Bonhoeffer was hanged, and Hitler was judged by the Judge of the universe. Allied forces – mainly the United States and Great Britain – fought Germany militarily, but it was Bonhoeffer who waged the battle for the soul of Germany. He was **convinced that it is both a Christian right and a Christian duty before God to oppose a government no longer obedient to the Laws of God.** This explains why Bonhoeffer was not a pacifist. He did all he could to urge others to join him in the resistance movement saying that the one who severs himself from the Confessional Church severs himself from the Grace of God. This may sound a bit judgmental to us spineless Americans, but Bonhoeffer understood spiritual warfare and knew that Liberty could not be won by the weak and timid. He saw an unbreakable connection between faith in Christ and faithfulness to Christ's cause. Christ's cause was Liberty – Liberty for the Church to preach Jesus Christ. An ideal Government is one which maintains Inalienable Rights and protects individual Freedoms. Socialism fails in this regard! So does a Monarchy where a king is invariably promoted who knows how to take Rights to himself and violate the Rights of his people.

The Ludgment of God against a nation must always be left in the hands of God. Sometimes it comes in the form of marauding bands of terrorists, as it was in the case of King Solomon; and sometimes it arrives as an Economic Depression; or it might appear as a domestic catastrophe, hurricanes, tornadoes or earthquakes; or it might come to us as an attack by a Foreign Power. In each of these possibilities, judgment is there to prompt us to repent and turn to the original pattern ordered by the Hand of Providence. We only have to read the Book of Jonah to see God's gracious intentions in the midst of Judgment.

We can never presume to know when God's judgment will be, whether immediate or delayed. The mercy of God is beyond anything we might imagine. I sat sickened at heart some time ago as I watched a Christian forum on TV, when one man said: **"I cannot wait to look down from heaven on all those miserable people left behind at the rapture!"** The thought of people left behind should make us weep – not rejoice! The deeper the sin in America, the more it becomes an occasion for the rescuing hand of God. Any Christian who has the Spirit of Jesus Christ will pray for a Deep and Great Awakening. How can we pray otherwise! This is why Jesus came into this world. This is why He sent the Holy Spirit. While we are looking at the depths of sin in America, may we turn and see the depths of God's love and delivering power. Can these bones live? Absolutely! Obviously, not by their own will-power! Hear the prophet share with us the heart of God: *"I will heal their apostasy! I will love them freely, for My anger has turned away."* [Hosea 14:4] May it be so! May it be so!

We now consider individuals and the Judgments of God. To repeat: **The Judgment of God is according to Existing Law.** God does not make it up as He

234

goes along, attempting to stay a step ahead of the man who is hopelessly stumbling. We as individuals are deeply advantaged: We not only have the Law of Nature and the Revealed Law of God, we also have Historic records of a multitude that preceded us; people who found that God never fails! Never!

The Law of Nature is referenced in Scripture. Paul told the Romans, *"For the wrath of God is revealed from heaven against all ungodliness and unrighteousness of men, who suppress the truth in unrighteousness, because that which is known about God is evident within them; for God made it evident to them. For since the creation of the world His invisible attributes – His eternal power and divine nature – have been clearly seen being understood through what has been made, so that they are without excuse."* [Romans 1:18-20; see also Romans 2:14-16]

Grace is loved by Christians, especially the nominal and the liberal! They see Grace as a free ticket to heaven, a complimentary pass into the riches at a spiritual sideshow with all kinds of bazaar benefits. There is no cost to the Christian for these freebees, they tell us; if there is, Jesus already paid the bill. Once this type of error gets into a culture's psyche, it is nigh impossible to root it out. Man would rather believe in a god who is half-blind than in the true God who sees flawlessly the motives of our hearts. Pastor Bonhoeffer faced this same death-producing problem in Germany, stating that Christians in that country **"have gathered like eagles round the carcass of cheap grace, and there we have drunk** of the poison which has killed the life of following Christ."[147]

When Jesus died on the Cross our salvation was purchased. The full price was paid by another. Bonhoeffer writes: **Behold the man sentenced by God, the figure of grief and pain. He is the Reconciler of the world. The guilt of mankind has fallen upon Him. It casts Him into shame and death before God's judgment seat. This is the great price which God pays for reconciliation with the world. Only by God's executing judgment upon Himself can there be peace between Him and the world.**[148] A man who wrongs another is expected to pay! But a man who wrongs God has nothing with which to pay. So it was that God Himself pays the debt that is owed to Him by man. Such is the Grace of God!

Scripture tells us that *He – who knew no sin – became sin for us.* [2 Cor.5:21] When He did He cried out on the Cross: *"My God! My God! Why have You forsaken Me?"* [Mark 15:34] The following scenario helps us understand the development of a right relationship with God:

1 **The primary sin of Man was to Forsake God in the Garden of Eden!**

2 **Jesus Christ took that particular sin and for that He was judged and forsaken by God!**

3 **Because Jesus was forsaken, Man no longer needs to be forsaking by God, for**

**Jesus bore that sin: Two Persons cannot
be charged with the same offense!**

4 **Because God no longer forsakes Man, Man
is invited to return and no longer forsake
God!**

5 **Herein is a secure and restful union between
God and Man, established by Jesus Christ
in His Death and Resurrection!**

Any preaching on Jesus Christ that excludes,
forgets or shuns these indispensable principles falls
short of God's desired objective. Jesus Christ is
the sole Redeemer of men. There is a host of self-
promoters and misleading speakers who seem bent
on promoting Eastern Religion as having something
to add to Jesus Christ. There is nothing that can be
added to the One who is all in all!

There was one principle instilled in Early
Americans, whether Christians or non-believers, a
principle that flowed out of the Great Awakening,
that **God was not to be offended!** This kept Colonial
society relatively wholesome. Scripture does tell us
that *"by the fear of the Lord men depart from evil."*
[Prov.16:6] Another result, already mentioned, was
that the Awakening compelled society to compose
and support a Declaration of Independence.

The singular wonder of Christianity is Jesus
Christ! Christianity is not a set of rules and regulations:
It is a Person with whom every true believer has a
personal relationship. The New Testament is like
a many-roomed mansion – every chapter holding
treasures for the researcher.

I would not have you unaware that a serious counterfeit Christianity has been offered to the American Church; it deserves our attention and, unless corrected, warrants God's Judgment. Bonhoeffer's Germany fell into the same spiritual ignorance and laziness, embracing cheap grace rather than relishing the riches of Christ's presence. Cheap grace lets the sinner stay unchanged while promising him heaven! Cheap grace justifies sin but not the sinner! Cheap grace is grace without discipline or the Cross! Cheap grace is grace without the Lordship of Jesus Christ! Cheap grace leaves a man lifeless, powerless and without fruit – and desperately in need of the life-changing breath of God!

The central figure of all history is Jesus Christ. Cheap grace moves the Lord aside and replaces Him with man, self-made man! For this the Judgment of God is right and proper. God said: *"I have installed My King!"* [Psalm 2:6; See 1 Tim.1:17; Heb.1:8] We may list a thousand errors, sins and blunders of man, but all of them fade into unimportance compared to that one deep offense – rejection of the Son of God. Other sins are forgivable. None of them can separate us from the love of God. There is one sin however that offends God to the point of judgment anger. That sin is the rejection of His Beloved Son. This is serious beyond words. And yet, He will forgive that sin too if we will but confess and forsake that sin! We humans are often urged to believe that we are the most precious treasure God could cherish. Not so! God's most treasured jewel is His own Son Jesus Christ! He loves Jesus so much that He gave Him the nations of the world for an inheritance, and the very ends of the earth as His possession. [Psalm 2:8]

The criminal hanging on a cross next to Jesus received forgiveness. Why? Because in one moment of time he said: *"Jesus, remember me when You enter Your Kingdom."* Jesus grace-filled response was: *"Today you shall be with Me in Paradise!"* [Luke 23:39-43] It will be better in the Judgment for the thief who met Jesus while on the cross than it will be for the outwardly moral person who gave $thousands to charity, or the politicians who gave public funds to the poor, or the preacher who offered his listeners some good ideas but never pressed on them the claims of Jesus Christ.

The writer of Hebrews tells us to *"lay aside every weight, and the sin which so easily entangles us, and let us run with diligence the race before us. Looking unto Jesus, the Author and Finisher of our faith . . ."* [Heb.12:1-2] It is impossible to say it to strongly, or repeat it too often, that Jesus is first in the Father's heart! Therefore, Jesus must be first in our hearts as well. Scripture tells us, *"the Father loves the Son . . ."* And: *"He who does not honor the Son does not honor the Father who sent Him."* [John 5:20, 23] *"Whoever denies the Son does not have the Father; the one who confesses the Son has the Father also."* [1 John 2:23] *". . . He who does not obey the Son shall not see life, but the wrath of God abides on him."* [John 3:36]

It is not my activities, my work for Him, my good intentions, my service, my donations, or even my desire to share truth with my neighbors that puts me in the good graces of God. That which pleases the Father is my love and devotion for His Son Jesus.

It was in the Garden of Eden where man broke off relations with God, choosing to be his own god. At that point man fell under the Judgment of God. Jesus came to earth to take upon Himself that Judgment, bringing man back into union with God. Jesus said: *"He who hears My word and believes Him who sent Me, has eternal life and will not come into Judgment, but has passed from death into life."* [John 5:24]

When Jesus Christ enters the life of anyone – everything changes! At that point the believer in Jesus is *"destined to be conformed to the image and likeness of God's Son."* [Rom.8:29] Because you have been rescued from the slave market of sin, Paul tells the believer, *"you belong to Christ . . . you have been bought with a price."* [1 Cor.3:23; 6:20] To make sure he got it, Paul says again, *"you have been bought with a price."* [1 Cor.7:23]

There is Judgment to come! Some will tremble and shake. Others will stand confident and sure, having come to know Jesus Christ personally as their Lord.

God made the first move on our behalf. He became guilty of our guilt, taking upon Himself the Judgment we earned. We are culpable, fully to blame for our sin of forsaking Him; and yet, that is the specific blame Jesus willingly took to Himself. The Father judged Him guilty that you and I might go free, that we might face the ultimate Judgment, and do it unafraid!

22 – THE LAMB OF GOD

The next day John the Baptist saw Jesus coming to him, and said: *"Behold, the Lamb of God who takes away the sin of the world."* - John 1:29

Sometimes words seem too few and weak
To picture Christ of Whom we speak.
    We're left with adjectives so frail;
    Words are important, but they fail
To capture all that we should say
About that first blessed Christmas Day!
    'Tis now two thousand years ago,
    God sent His Son that we might know
The peace that He alone can give
To us – once dead, though now we live.

'Tis more than nouns or verbs or words;
It's more than what our ears have heard;
    'Tis more than what our eyes can see,
For He fills all eternity!
John said, "If books the world filled
They could not adequately build
    A picture perfect of our Lord:
    They'd earn no wonderful award!"
Somehow — beyond what ears can hear
We must meet Him that much is clear.

But how can we — frail, sinful men —
Come to this spotless One, and then
    Be not consumed by purity;
    Instead, live on eternally?
Could this be so? Dare I believe
A sinful child of sinful Eve
    Could walk again with God above?
    Is there within His heart such love?
Or — must I wander aimlessly,
An outcast for eternity?

'Tis here all human logics fail,
For man's too ignorant and frail:
    If God's so far beyond our realm —
    His holiness to overwhelm
The very best of upright men —
How can I fellowship again?
    God made a way! That's what He said
    To shepherds as their sheep they fed:
"Peace on the earth! Good will to men!"
And angels echoed back: *"Amen!"*

But how can such a message be
Good now and for eternity?
    How can the coming of a Child
    Deliver me, by sin defiled?
Is there a key I'm missing here?
What will it take to make it clear?
    — Perhaps it's not the Babe at all
    Who'll rescue me from Adam's fall!
God's promise, no, is not a sham,
For Christ became God's chosen Lamb.

"I lay My life down on My own!"
That's what He said. And all alone
   He paid the price that I should pay
   On that — God's awful judgment day;
When on God's Son my sin was laid;
And on the Cross my debt was paid.
   Oh, now I see! That's why He came
   To take my blame – my sin – my shame!
"You took the Judgment meant for me!
I'll live my life, Lord, just for Thee!"

23 – THE CHRISTIAN AND POLITICS

An earnest Christian said to me: **"I don't vote! I'm not a part of this world: My home is in heaven. I let the world take care of itself."** I wonder how the Founders would have answered that reluctant attitude! I wonder what Patrick Henry, or Samuel Adams, or Peter Muhlenberg would say! I wonder what his children will say when the Judgment of God comes and the Christian lets the world run itself into empty chaos.

John Jay, an ardent Christian, was appointed by Pres. George Washington to be the first Chief Justice of the Supreme Court. Jay said: **"Providence has given to our people the choice of their rulers, and it is the duty, as well as the privilege and interest of our Christian nation to select and prefer Christians for their rulers."**[150]

The benefit and value of a Christian's involvement in politics rests in the motive. Dietrich Bonhoeffer gives this advice: **"The fanatic believes that he can oppose the power of evil with the purity of his will and of his principle. Even if his fanaticism serves the right cause of truth or justice, he will sooner or later become entangled with non-essentials and petty details and fall into the snare set by his more skillful opponent."** Later Bonhoeffer writes: **"Radicalism always springs from a conscious or unconscious hatred of what is established. Christian radicalism, no matter whether it consists in withdrawing from the world or in improving the world, arises from hatred of creation."** When a man is at peace with God, and has found spiritual rest, he loves what the Son of God loves – and God loves the world [John 3:16]: He does not condemn it [John 3:17].

Bonhoeffer reasons that we can neither be radical in our approach to the mammoth political issues of the day, nor withdraw into isolation, live our private lives according to our good conscience, and passively let the world go to ruin. **We have a duty that can only be effective in God.** Bonheoffer tells us that if I am prone to arbitrary and enthusiastic action I must not confuse that natural impulse with the call of Jesus. On the other hand, if I am cautious and timid and law-abiding, then I must guard against thinking the will of Jesus always falls within those restrictive confines.

The Great Awakening had liberated the Colonists from the old tensions and factions of Europe, and brought them into a commitment to each other. But more importantly, they were committed to Jesus Christ. Had they been simply natural men obeying the natural impulse to simply do their own thing – there never would have been an America! Christ Himself was the Architect and Builder who directed the American experiment, doing so through the lives of those who willingly obeyed Him, some, to the point of death.

How things have changed—not just in that we have switched foundations in America. A more vital change is in the attitude of Christians toward politics. In Colonial days it was the Christian who grappled with political issues, making sure legislation was in accord with God's Law. Today too many Christians prefer to wait for Jesus to return to straighten out the mess. The following Twelve Steps are given to show how a factual rendering of the Constitution crumbled into a liberal reading of that Document:

1 Mayflower Compact, which lasted over 70 years, was the first "constitution" in America, written **"for the glory of God."**

2 Providential miracles: Spanish Armada defeated—1588; French Fleet destroyed—1746; George Washington preserved in French-Indian Wars—1755; and many, many more.

3 The Great Awakening of the 1740s – a spiritual movement that changed the hearts of Colonialists, multiplied the churches and altered Colonial culture, released society from British influence, preparing it for nationhood.

4 Declaration of Independence, July 2, 1776.

5 Articles of Confederation [Ratified, 1777; Effective, 1781], a friendship but powerless agreement between the Colonies. It had no authorization to maintain an army, no power to pass laws binding upon individuals, and adopted no uniform monetary system. This led to—

6 The U.S. Constitution [Approved 1787; Effective 1789], enacted by **"We the People. . ."** and based on the Law of Nature. This was

the **"bones"** of our legal system, replacing the ineffective Articles of Confederation.

7 Bill of Rights – the first ten amendments effective 1791. Here is the **"meat"** being added to the bones! Other amendments were adopted from time to time.

8 Various State Documents that referenced God: "<u>**New Hampshire 1792**</u> – *Every individual has a natural and unalienable right to worship God according to the dictates of his own conscience.* <u>New Jersey 1844</u> – *We, the people of the State of New Jersey, grateful to Almighty God for civil and religious liberty which He hath so long permitted us to enjoy, and looking to Him for a blessing on our endeavors.* <u>New Mexico 1911</u> – *We, the People of New Mexico, grateful to Almighty God for the blessings of liberty.* <u>New York 1846</u> – *We, the people of the State of New York, grateful to Almighty God for our freedom, in order to secure its blessings.*"

9 Early on the Courts define the United States as a Christian nation, but continued to rule as though America was a secular nation.

10 Secular writers suggested that the Constitution was a living document. That is, it was adaptable to modern times; it was flexible and changeable as the courts saw fit. Chief Justice Hughes' remark was fitting: **"The Constitution is what the judges say it is."**

11 Interpretive Freedom – This included both strict and loose constructionism. Both used

the Constitution as their base: Conservatives hold closely to the letter of the Constitution, while liberals apply the Constitution with relative laxity. This is seen in the Roe v Wade decision, as well as the school integration rulings, neither of which is found based in the Constitution.

12 Noninterpretivism – While interpretivism rests its case on the Constitution, non-interpretivism looks outside of the Constitution for judicial wisdom, preferring to not be bound by the text of the Constitution. Instead of deciding what the Constitution means, noninterpretivism decides what it **SHOULD** mean, or what the judges **WANT** it to mean. Under this scheme of things there is no end to the foolish results. The professed objective is to see the Constitution as an evolutionary document, untied to the text or the original meaning; the ultimate result will be that the already devalued Constitution may be eliminated from American life if liberal political thinkers have their way.

USA Today, July 7, 2003, reported that "Supreme Court Justice Anthony Kennedy cited foreign law in the landmark case [*Lawrence vs. Texas*]. Writing for the majority . . . Justice Anthony Kennedy noted that the European Court of Human Rights and other foreign courts have affirmed the 'rights of homosexual adults to engage in intimate, consensual conduct.' Never**

before had the Supreme Court's majority cited a foreign legal precedent in such a big case. Kennedy's opinion in *Lawrence vs. Texas*, which was signed by four other justices, has ignited a debate among analysts over whether it was a signal that the justices will adopt foreign courts' views of individual liberties." The two justices most interested in accepting foreign legal trends are Ginsburg and Breyer.

While this judicial deviation takes place in the justice system, something similar is happening in the Church. Lawyers and judges leap over the Constitution, back to a foreign, non-Christian legal system. At the same time the Church leaps over the Bible, back to the mystic fathers, Eastern Religion, Islam and other non-Christian cultures. The *"modern"* Christian says **"We have moved beyond the old doctrines and age-worn creeds of the past. The Church is progressing! We know better how to do church than Paul did!"** This type of statement – uttered in my own hearing – is usually conceived in Charismatic circles and brought to birth in the present-day Church Growth Movement and the Emerging church.

As society fell away from God, there was but one hope left to man: A Great Awakening! At the time of the Revolution and well into the mid-1800s, the preacher's Sunday sermon was published in the Monday morning newspaper for the whole town to read. There was a genuine hunger for restoration! As people read the Sunday sermon, the local preacher, not the lawyers, became the one who set the standard for morality in the community. The Church grew in influence, not because of a man-planned program, but because people were desperate to be right with God. The judiciary fell in line with the righteous teachings of the Church because of the Church's powerful impact on the culture. When the Spirit of God again breathes into existence a Great Awakening of America, man's relations with God will be restored. And the Law of God will serve the culture as it once did. **Can these bones live? Lord! Thou knowest!**

As for our non-voting Christian friend, he may contend that America is no longer a Christian nation, and therefore deserves to be deserted by the Church and by God. To which we can only say that the Lord God's question to Ezekiel comes through faint but clear: *"Can these bones live?"* Despite Israel's move away from God, they were not abandoned. God still cared enough to give Ezekiel a vision of what he could look forward to—a valley of dry bones coming together, clothed with flesh, living, and a mighty army.

Can these bones live? We may not be prepared to boldly say *Yes!* But, we dare not say *No!* For we thereby deny the power and passion of Jesus Christ for the world, a world He does not hate, a world He loves, a world for which He died [John 3:16-17; 2 Cor.5:19].

Note: Watch for the sequel, due out in autumn, 2009. *DPP*

End Notes

~~~

1   Verna M. Hall, _The Christian History of the Constitution_: Christian Self-Government (San Francisco: Foundation for American Christian Education, 1966) p.Ia.

2   _1828 Dictionary of the English Language_ ~ NP (Providence defined).

3   Peter Marshall & David Manuel, _The Light and the Glory_ (Old Tappan, NJ: Fleming H. Revell, 1977) p.17.

4   John Foxe, Foxe's Christian Martyrs of the World (Westwood, NJ: Barbour & Company, c.1565) pp.510-11,

5   _Messages & Papers of the Presidents_, Vol.1, p.44.

6   Henry Wadsworth Longfellow, _The Complete Poetical Works of Henry Wadsworth Longfellow_ (NY: Grosset & Dunlap, 1841) p.273. Longfellow's Poem, The Ballad of the French Fleet, was written in 1887, 140 years after the event.

7 William J. Federer, *America's God and Country*, (Coppell, TX: Fame Publishing, Inc.) p.636.

8 Ibid., pp.636-37; & *The Light & the Glory*, pp.285-86.

9 *The Light & the Glory*, pp.342-43.

10 Edward Dumbauld, Ed., *The Political Writings of Thomas Jefferson* [New York: The Liberal Arts Press, 1955] p.98.

11 William J. Federer, *America's God and Country* (Coppell, TX: Fame Publishing, Inc, 1994} p.391

12 *The Rebirth of America* (Arthur S. DeMoss Foundation, 1986) p.41.

13 Forrest McDonald & Ellen Shapiro McDonald, *Requiem* (Univ. Press of Kansas, 1988) p.1-2

14 Noah Webster, *1828 American Dictionary of the English Language* (San Francisco: Foundation for American Christian Education, 1967) Education defined.

15 *Desk Book, American Jurisprudence 2d* (Rochester, NY: The Lawyers Co-operative Publishing Company, 1962) p.54.

16 James D. Richardson, U.S. House of Repr., *Messages and Papers of the Presidents*, (NY: Bureau of National Literature, 1911) Vol.1, p.58.

17 Verna M. Hall, *The Christian History of the American Revolution* (San Francisco: Foundation for American Christian Education, 1967) pp.614-15.

18 *The Rebirth of America*, p.127.

19   James D. Richardson, Editor, *Messages & Papers of the Presidents* (NY: Bureau of National Literature, 1897) p.212.

20   *1828 American Dictionary of the English Language*, p.12.

21   *America's God and Country*, pp.10-11.

22   *http://en.wikiquote.org/wiki/Samuel_Adams*

23   Edward Dumbauld, *The Political Writings of Thomas Jefferson* (NY: The Liberal Arts Press, 1955) p.190.

24   Forrest McDonald, *Novus Ordo Seclorum* (Univ. Press of Kansas, 1985) p.48

25   *Message & Papers of the Presidents*, p.56.

26   *America's God and Country*, p.325.

27   A Deist is one who believes that God created all things, but no longer has a relationship to his world. Like an absentee landlord, he has no contact with the world, there is no revelation of His will given to man, and no Savior necessary. Man will ultimately be eternally judged on the basis of his deeds.

28   Forrest McDonald, *A Constitutional History of the United States* (Malabar, FL: Robert E. Krieger Publ. Co., 1982) pp.12-13.

29   *Requiem,* p.6.

30   Ibid., p.7.

31   Jones' Blackstone, *Commentaries on the Laws of England* (Baton Rouge: Claitor's Publishing Division, 1976 [Originally Published in 1765) p.54.

32   *America's God and Country*, p.397.

33 Charles G. Finney, *Lectures on Systematic Theology* (Grand Rapids, MI: Wm B. Eerdmans Publ. Co., 1957) p.221.

34 *Jones' Blackstone*, Vol.1, pp.64–65.

35 *Am Jur 2d Desk Book*, 1962 Edition, p.54.

36 *The Political Writings of Thomas Jefferson*, p.82

37 *History of the Christian Church*, p.125.

38 *http://en.wikipedia.org/wiki/Salvian*

39 *History of the Christian Church*, p.128.

40 *America's God and Country*, p.323.

41 *Messages & Papers of the Presidents.*, Vol.1, p.212

42 *Requiem*, p.12.

43 *The Light & the Glory*, p.284–85.

44 *America's God and Country*, p.318.

45 *The Rebirth of America*, p.39.

46 *1828 American Dictionary of the English Language*, p.13.

47 *Maxims of George Washington*, p.186.

48 *1828 American Dictionary of the English Language* ~ NP ~ [Savage Defined]

49 Ibid., NP [Christian Defined]

50 http://www.independent.org/publications/article.asp?id=1329

51 *America's God and Country*, pp.108–09.

52 *Novus Ordo Seclorum*, pp.70–71.

53 *America's God and Country*, p.98.

54 Baron Montesquieu [1689-1755] wrote *The Spirit of Laws* in which he said: ***God is related to the universe, as Creator and Preserver; the laws by which He created all things are those***

by which He preserves them. He also said that *the Catholic Religion is most agreeable to a Monarchy, and the Protestant to a Republic.* [See John Eidsmoe's *Christianity and the Constitution*, pp.54-56]

55   John Locke [1632-1704] was a British political writer who wrote *The Reasonableness of Christianity* as well as a *Treatise on Civil Government*, the latter dealing with everything from War, Slavery, Property, Family, Government, Tyranny, etc. [See Verna Hall's *Christian Self-Government*, publ. by *Foundation for American Christian Education*, San Francisco, pp.57-125.

56   *The Cost of Discipleship*, p.26 [Memoir, G. Leibholz]

57   House of Representatives, The *Two Hundredth Anniversary of the First Continental Congress*, 1774-1974 (Washington DC: United States Government Printing Office, 1975) pp.46-55.

58   Ibid., p.52.

59   *The Light and the Glory*, p.258.

60   Hon. Philip M. Crane, *The Sum of Good Government* (Ottawa, IL: Green Hills Publishers 1976) p.4.

61   *The Political Writings of Thomas Jefferson*, p.30.

62   *Pennsylvania Supreme Court*, Wallace v. Harmstad, 1863.

63   *America's God and Country*, p.562.

64 Edmund Burke, *Conciliation With America* (Boston: Ginn & Company, 1897) pp.24-25, 31.

65 *The Light and the Glory*, p.264

66 Ibid., pp.264-65.

67 Samuel Rutherford, *Lex Rex* (Harrisonburg, VA: Sprinkle Publications, 1982 [Orig. Printing: 1644]) p.xix.

68 *The Light and the Glory*, p.266.

69 *Ethics*, pp.100-09.

70 Ibid., pp.98-99.

71 *America's God and Country*, p.245.

72 John Eidsmoe, *Christianity and the Constitution* (Grand Rapids, MI: Baker Book House, 1987) p.52.

73 Alan Heimert & Perry Miller, *The Great Awakening* (Indianapolis: The Bobbs - Merrill Co, 1967), pp.184-86.

74 Ibid., p.184.

75 Alan Heimert & Perry Miller, *The Great Awakening* (NY: The Bobbs - Merrill Company, 1967) This book is the foundation for the information in this section on the Religious Awakening in America. Pages 20-34 covers Jonathan Edwards' analysis of a spiritual awakening.

76 *The Light and the Glory*, p.309.

77 *America's God and Country*, p.20.

78 Ibid., p.204-05.

79 Francis Schaeffer, *How Should We Then Live?* (Old Tappan, NJ: Fleming H. Revell, 1976) p.122.

80   Rousas J. Rushdoony, *This Independent Republic* (Fairfax, VA: Thoburn Press, 1978) pp.24-25.
81   Patrick Henry's speech on Liberty was delivered to a Virginia Delegation on March 28, 1775, and greatly moved the Colonies toward Independence. Full speech recorded in America's God and Country, p.288.
82   *The Light & the Glory*, p.309.
83   *America's God and Country*, p.20.
84   Ibid., p.274.
85   M.E. Bradford, *A Worthy Company* (Plymouth: Plymouth Rock Foundation, 1982) p.viii.
86   *Messages & Papers of the Presidents*, Vol.1, pp.212-13.
87   Henry Wadsworth Longfellow, *The Complete Poetical Works of Henry Wadsworth Longfellow* (New York: Grosset & Dunlap Publ., 1841) pp.183-84.
88   *America's God and Country*, p.503.
89   Ibid., p.500.
90   Ibid., p.505.
91   Alexander Hamilton, James Madison, John Jay, The Federalist Papers (NY: New American Library, 1961) pp. 230-31.
92   *Webster's 1828 Dictionary of the English Language*, p.12.
93   Ibid., p.20
94   *Ethics*, pp. 71, 241.
95   *America's God and Country*, p.641.
96   *America's God and Country*, p.288.
97   Ibid., p.289.

98 John Wm. Richards, How *Lutherans Helped Win Liberty* (Columbus, OH: The Lutheran Book Concern, 1927) The information in this chapter is derived from Richards' book.

99 *The Cost of Discipleship*, p.330 [Footnote].

100 Harry V. Jaffa, *How to Think About the American Revolution* (Durham, NC: Carolina Academic Press, 1978) p.52.

101 William H. McGuffey, *The Original McGuffey's, The Eclectic First Reader* (Cincinnati: Truman and Smith, 1836) pp.95-96. [The Original McGuffey's is a trademark of Mott Media, Inc., the re-publisher of McGuffey's Readers: They are located at 1000 East Huron, Milford, Michigan 48042].

102 *www.khouse.org/articles/2001/365/*.

103 *The Leipzig Connection*, pp.24-26

104 Rosalie J. Slater, Teaching and Learning America's Christian History: The Principle Approach (San Francisco: Foundation for American Christian Education, 1965) pp. xvi-xvii.

105 Verna Hall, *The Christian History of the American Revolution: Consider and Ponder* {San Francisco: Foundation for American Christian Education, 1976) p.615.

106 *America's God and Country*, pp.10-11.

107 Ibid., p.543.

108 *The Rebirth of America*, p.127.

109 *http://www.anevangelicalmanifesto.com/docs/* [This site opens to an Index of Topics where is found Evangelical Manifesto.

110   David Pett, *Christian Heritage Manual*, (Clackamas, OR: CHF, ND) p.43 [Page 34 in Tucker's *Constitutional Law*].

111   *Ethics*, p.170.

112   *America's God and Country*, p.288.

113   Editorial Board, *Webster Comprehensive Dictionary* (Chicago: J.G. Ferguson Publishing Company, 1986) p.436.

114   *Ethics*, p.17.

115   *America's God and Country*, p.561.

116   Ibid, p.560.

117   *Ethics*, p.309, 335.

118   *America's God and Country*, p.500.

119   *Maxims of George Washington*, pp.139, 143.

120   *Jones' Blackstone*, pp.220-21.

121   *http://www.lighthousetrailsresearch.com/wilkinsonquits.htm*

122   *America's God and Country*, p.222.

123   Ibid., p.101.

124   Ibid., p.602.

125   *Acts 4:19-20*. Peter was an outstanding witness for Jesus Christ, considering the fact that he had a few days earlier denied even knowing Jesus. Now, being full of the Spirit of God, Jesus is his full and final authority.

126   *America's God and Country*, p.560.

127   *The Federalist Papers*, pp.38, 230-31.

128   America's God and Country, p.602.

129   *Ethics*, p.297.

130   Ibid., p.291. These comments were written by Bonhoeffer when Hitler was gaining power and increasingly in his opposition to the Church.

Truths like these eventually led to Bonhoeffer's hanging at a direct command from Hitler. Hitler did not fulfill God's Mandate, and it was right for Bonhoeffer to oppose him – though it cost him his life.

131 *The Great Awakening*, p.29.

132 *http://www.aboutabortions.com/Confess.html.*

133 *Ethics*, p.342.

134 *America's God and Country*, p.500.

135 Ibid., p.5.

136 *Ethics*, p.66.

137 *http://homepages.which.net/~radical.faith/ thought/bonhoeffer.htm*

138 *The Cost of Discipleship*, p.25

139 Roger Manvell & Heinrich Fraenkel, *The Canaris Conspiracy*, 1969 (NY: Pinnacle Books) p.265.

140 Ibid., p.263.

141 Joachim Fest, Trans. by Bruce Little: *Plotting Hitler's Death* (NY: Metropolitan Books, 1996) p.25.

142 Ibid., p.18.

143 The Canaris Conspiracy, p.268.

144 Ibid., p.270.

145 Francis A Schaeffer: *The Great Evangelical Disaster* (Wheaton: Crossway Books, 1984) p.25.

146 *Systematic Theology*, p.221.

147 *The Cost of Discipleship*, p.57.

148 *Ethics*, p.75.

149 Ibid., p.318.

150 *Ethics*, pp.66, 129.

Printed in the United States
208231BV00001B/115-315/P

9 781606 479780